About the Author

Professor Brian Boyd is Reader in Education at the University of Strathclyde. He has previously been a teacher of English, a head teacher and Chief Adviser in Strathclyde. He has published widely in the academic press and educational journals, and is a frequent contributor to conferences on a range of educational issues. He is co-founder of Tapestry, an educational organisation whose aim is to promote new thinking about learning and teaching. He used to play on the right wing for Port Glasgow Juniors.

Foreword

The *Times Educational Supplement Scotland* is delighted to be associated with the publication of this prestigious new series of books devoted to key areas in the field of continuing professional development.

Since the newspaper's birth in 1965, we have always attempted to inform, educate, and occasionally entertain the Scottish teaching profession, as well as to encourage dialogue between all educational sectors. In recent years, our commitment to the concept of encouraging educationists to constantly reflect – and act – upon best practice has been most tangibly evident in the provision of an annual CPD supplement. This offers full and detailed examination of developments in CPD from both Scottish and international contexts, and we attempt to share best practice in a manner that is both accessible and valuable.

This series of books is another testimony of our commitment to CPD. Drawing on the experience of foremost Scottish practitioners, each book attempts to offer academic rigour with a lightness of delivery that is too often found wanting in the weightier tomes that populate many educational libraries, and which are consequently left unread, except by those approaching examinations – or job interviews.

In short, we hope that these books will be welcomed in the groves of academe; but we also believe that they deserve to be read – and acted upon – by a much wider audience: those teachers across Scotland, nursery, primary and secondary, who deliver the curriculum on a daily basis to our young people.

Neil Munro
Editor, *Times Educational Supplement Scotland*

continuing professional development in education

CPD: Improving Professional Practice

An introduction to CPD for teachers

Brian Boyd

Series editor: Brian Boyd
Published in association with the
Times Educational Supplement Scotland

Hodder Gibson

A MEMBER OF THE HODDER HEADLINE GROUP

The Publishers would like to thank the following for permission to reproduce copyright material:

Acknowledgements

From Winnie-the-Pooh © A.A. Milne. Published by Egmont UK Limited, London and used with permission.

From The House at Pooh Corner © A.A. Milne. Published by Egmont UK Limited, London and used with permission.

From The Tao of Pooh © Benjamin Hoff. Published by Egmont UK Limited, London and used with permission.

Every effort has been made to trace all copyright holders, but if any have been inadvertently overlooked the Publishers will be pleased to make the necessary arrangements at the first opportunity.

Although every effort has been made to ensure that website addresses are correct at time of going to press, Hodder Gibson cannot be held responsible for the content of any website mentioned in this book. It is sometimes possible to find a relocated web page by typing in the address of the home page for a website in the URL window of your browser.

Orders: please contact Bookpoint Ltd, 130 Milton Park, Abingdon, Oxon OX14 4SB. Telephone: (44) 01235 827720. Fax: (44) 01235 400454. Lines are open 9.00–6.00, Monday to Saturday, with a 24-hour message answering service. Visit our website at www.hoddereducation.co.uk. Hodder Gibson can be contacted direct on: Tel: 0141 848 1609; Fax: 0141 889 6315; email: hoddergibson@hodder.co.uk

© Brian Boyd 2005
First published in 2005 by
Hodder Gibson, a member of the Hodder Headline Group
2a Christie Street
Paisley PA1 1NB

Impression number   10 9 8 7 6 5 4 3 2 1
Year   2010 2009 2008 2007 2006 2005

Cover illustration by David Parkin.
Typeset by Transet Limited, Coventry, England.
Printed and bound in Great Britain by CPI Bath

A catalogue record for this title is available from the British Library

ISBN-10: 0-340-88991-8
ISBN-13: 978-0-340-88991-6

Contents

1 CPD – what's in a name?

> By the time it came to the edge of the Forest the stream had grown up, so that it was almost a river, and, being grown-up, it did not run and jump and sparkle as it used to do when it was younger, but moved more slowly. For it knew where it was going, and it said to itself, 'There is no hurry. We shall get there some day.'
>
> *The Tao of Pooh*, B. Hoff

Enter the dragon – the emergence of CPD

Let's imagine, just for a moment, that you are at the doctor's. You enter the surgery, your name is called and the doctor ushers you into the room. In the few minutes of introductory chat, before diagnosis begins, the doctor volunteers the information that he has been qualified for 30 years. In that time, he states proudly, he has never read a single book on medicine. Not only that, he never gets involved in field trials of new medicines or drugs and avoids training courses with other GPs like the plague. The best way of being a good doctor is to sharpen your skills 'on the job'. How would you feel? Would you be thinking of changing your doctor or even moving to a new practice?

Well, school pupils don't usually have that choice and rarely, if ever, know whether their teachers take part in in-service training, keep up to date in their reading about the theory and practice of teaching or take any account of research. Until very recently, it was possible for teachers to avoid in-service training, or, at least, to regard pre-service training – in the main, one year for secondary and four for primary teachers – as enough to equip them for a career of 30 to 40 years in the classroom. 'Experience' would do the rest. Indeed, there was a certain cynicism about 'theory' and anyone – advisers, teacher educators or researchers –

who claimed to be able to deliver in-service training, was looked upon with suspicion.

Momentous changes have taken place which influenced the curriculum or assessment (e.g. *The Primary Memorandum*, 1965 or *Munn* and *Dunning*, 1977), altered the structure of schooling (comprehensive schools, 1965) or changed the nature of the pupil population (the Raising of the School Leaving Age, 1971/72) and teachers were expected to cope with the minimum of preparation. Indeed, for ROSLA, all secondary school staff in Scotland were allowed four early closures over a month and watched television programmes designed to prepare them for a new cohort of fifteen to sixteen-year-olds, many of whom resented having to stay on an extra year, and for whom there was little in the way of an appropriate curriculum!

The situation began to change in the 1980s, principally as a result of pressure from teacher unions and as a consequence of Government-led initiatives such as TVEI, which had money attached to them to ensure that change would happen quickly and which targeted in-service training as one way of ensuring that teachers assimilated new ideas.

The introduction of five in-service days per year (still known in England and Wales as 'Baker days' in reference to the Conservative Education Minister who introduced them), the devolution of funding firstly to local authorities rather than colleges of education in-service departments and then, subsequently, to schools themselves, upped the ante. The quality of training, its relevance to the schools' development plans and its cost-effectiveness became important considerations. The old idea of the 'command economy' where the Scottish Office Education Department or local authorities would decide, from the centre, what teachers needed and would then engage college lecturers to 'deliver' it, began to change. Schools could now engage whoever they wanted to, within reason, from other authorities, from the growing number of private educational consultants or the university education faculties to do in-service training with staff. Authorities could do likewise, and, as the number of advisers began to diminish in the mid 1990s after local government reorganisation, their role was to act as brokers, trying to ensure that they provided a programme for teachers and schools which benefited from economies of scale.

Fullan and Hargreaves have argued that:

...it is only in the last few years that teacher development as a concept has come under scrutiny. In so doing, it has become clear that previous assumptions about linking staff development and effective change confined to specific innovations were too limited. We now begin to see that comprehensive career-long teacher development and institutional reforms in faculties of education and school systems is the real agenda. Teacher development is thus positioned to take a central role in educational reform in the 1990s.

(1993: p. 8)

Now, albeit a decade later, *A Teaching Profession for the 21st Century* (The Scottish Executive Education Department 2001) has enshrined the notion of Continuing Professional Development (CPD) within teachers' contracts. It is both an entitlement and a requirement for every teacher to engage in at least 35 CPD hours' over and above the five in-service days and any other in-service training carried out within the school day. Every teacher must maintain a CPD portfolio, and must discuss it with a line manager within the school. CPD has undoubtedly arrived!

CPD – more than a change in terminology?

As in many aspects of education, terminology has changed throughout the years, reflecting the mood or orthodoxy of the moment. 'In-service training' has long been the term used by most teachers. The word 'training' was not thought problematic, since, after all, teachers had undergone 'teacher training', sometimes known as 'pre-service training'. Indeed, the Colleges of Education in which the training took place, had 'In-service Departments'. In the 1980s, the word 'training' was challenged as Colleges of Education began the process of merging with universities and became Faculties of Education. The 'Professional Development Unit' replaced the In-service Department in the Faculty of Education of Strathclyde University (formerly Jordanhill College of Education) and around the same time Teacher Training became 'Initial Teacher Education'. Thus, 'training', with its connotations of apprenticeships, skills and subject knowledge was replaced by 'professional development', emphasising reflection, professionalism and pedagogy.

The phrase 'staff development' became current in the 1990s, often in conjunction with the term 'review'. Staff development and review was, in some respects, a euphemism for staff development and appraisal, a highly contentious notion introduced by Michael Forsyth, Conservative Education Minister in the 1990s. The teaching profession reacted strongly to what they saw as the imposition of a top-down, bureaucratic and punitive method of judging their performance. They were suspicious of a potential link between appraisal and performance-related pay and deeply resistant to a civil service model of appraisal which they felt took no account of their professionalism. Thus, faced with downright refusal from teachers to engage in appraisal schemes, many local authorities in the 1990s agreed staff development and review schemes with the teaching unions. Notwithstanding this softly-softly approach, by the time the McCrone committee was set up in 2000, some authorities had schools where less than 50 per cent of the staff had agreed to be involved in the staff development and review schemes.

A Teaching Profession for the 21st Century established a new contractual context for professional review and development. It required that 'teachers shall have an ongoing commitment to maintain their professional expertise through an agreed programme of continuing professional development'. The acronym CPD was introduced early in the report and has become the shorthand which everyone uses:

> ...every teacher will have an annual Continuing Professional Development (CPD) plan agreed with her/his immediate manager and every teacher will be required to maintain an individual CPD record.
>
> (2001: p. 16)

Thus, we now have 'CPD' as the official term, while 'in-service' days and 'staff development' co-ordinators still remain in schools. The terminology remains confused but, in a real sense, CPD rules!

What counts as CPD?

Ask most teachers and they will say that CPD is about courses and events, sometimes in-school, during in-service days, but usually in some central location, perhaps a teachers' centre, an education faculty, or, (rarely if you are an ordinary classroom teacher) in a hotel. The leader/facilitator will be an adviser or lecturer or sometimes a 'guru', according to Michael Fullan – a term used because the user can't spell charlatan! The participants may or may not have had any choice about attending and may or may not feel that the course is relevant to their needs. Just as there were teachers who avoided in-service training at all costs, so too were there professional course-goers, teachers who volunteered for every course on offer and whose classroom practice seemed, miraculously, to continue unaffected!

CPD now embraces a much wider range of activities and experiences. The Scottish Executive has issued a list which it claims is 'intended to be illustrative rather than exhaustive':

- Activity related to achieving national standards (Standard for Full Registration, Standard for Chartered Teacher, Standard for Headship).
- Self-evaluation and personal reflection including preparation for the professional review and development meeting.
- Subject-based activities including involvement with professional bodies and associations.
- Attendance at in-service training.
- Membership of school committees and task groups.
- Developing school, local authority and national policies.
- Visits to and from colleagues in other schools.
- Co-operative teaching.
- Lesson observation and analysis.
- Secondments.
- Professional reading and research.
- Mentoring/supporting colleagues.
- Curricular planning/development.
- Management and leadership development opportunities.
- Teacher placements.
- Working with others including as part of inter-agency teams involving colleagues from social work, health service, etc.
- Working with parents/carers.

(2002: p. 7)

So, it is not only a change of name! It is a complete re-think of what constitutes CPD. It recognises what many teachers who were already 'reflective professionals' have been doing, often in their own time, without any official recognition. It would have been inconceivable to a previous generation of teachers that 'professional reading and research' should be part of their ongoing professional development. And 'lesson observation and analysis' for some teachers would have been a step too far, an intrusion into their, and colleagues', classrooms.

CPD – reactions from the profession

Early reaction to the broadening of CPD boundaries and to its status as an entitlement have been varied. Purdon (2003) has argued that 'much of the consultation on CPD-related matters provides evidence that the majority opinion supports the development of a CPD 'framework'.' She suggests that:

> Through CPD, teachers have the opportunity to become even better at what they do, to try new approaches, to develop and to share new ideas about the nature and purpose of teaching.
>
> (2003: p. 951)

Christie (2003: p. 958) links the concept of 'professional standards' with accountability and argues that the recommendations of the McCrone Committee represent a 'recognition of the importance of continuing professional development (CPD), both as a professional entitlement and as a professional obligation'. Christie describes the elaborate consultation process, involving questionnaires to 60,000 teachers, which accompanied the development of the Standard for Chartered Teacher (a new post created by the McCrone Committee) and which resulted in general agreement on nine forms of 'professional action', including 'evaluate practice and reflect critically on it', 'improve professional performance' and 'ensure that teaching is informed by reading and research' (2003: p. 960).

In England and Wales, a report for the Department for Education and Skills (DfES Hustler *et al.*, 2003), revealed that older teachers are often cynical that in-service training-days are often used to promote government priorities. However, the survey also revealed that teachers value any kind of professional development, except for the poor training offered on using information technology. The survey, carried out by a team from Manchester Metropolitan University and Education Data Services, elicited 2,500 responses from primary, secondary and special educational needs teachers, and suggested that attitudes vary considerably between and within schools, and according to the gender, age and responsibilities of teachers. Newly qualified teachers and secondary school teachers were more likely to do courses 'out of personal interest'. While women were more likely to focus on teaching skills and subject knowledge, men tended to concentrate on their professional, leadership and management skills. Overall, primary teachers did most CPD while special educational needs teachers were most likely to complain about the lack of training tailored to their needs. It was reported that around 70 per cent of inset days were provided in-house but teachers gave higher ratings to training delivered by external consultants.

In a twenty-page pull-out supplement on CPD in May 2004, *The Times Educational Supplement Scotland* documented the way in which five teachers used their 35 hours CPD in the previous school session. They ranged from a second-year class teacher to one who had been teaching for 30 years. The range was impressive, from subject-based in-service, to initiatives such as Assessment is for Learning, to personal interests such as digital photography, to be used to record pupils' work. Some had taken part in local authority working groups or pilot projects, while others had embarked on national schemes such as the GTCS teacher researcher programme. Some of the teachers reported favourably on the process of maintaining their CPD folder, arguing that:

> it makes you appreciate how much you've been doing and encourages you to recognise that a lot of the reading that you do on teaching and learning ideas is relevant, valued and adding to your professionalism.
>
> (*TESS* May 2004)

For others, involvement in a single project can take up the whole 35 hours, working with colleagues, with pupils and attending courses. Finally, the opportunities offered by the Authority are key elements of the CPD experience. Many Authorities offer a wide range of courses from twilight, to weekend to vacation mode. The fact that most of these courses are free for the school makes it easier for them to support staff. Cover is not required and the school CPD budget is not compromised.

It would appear that since CPD is at the heart of most of the developments designed to improve schools, raise pupil attainment and make the teaching profession one which is attractive to new recruits, its future is secure. However, the views of the majority of teachers may be more complex and equivocal than the five in the *TESS* sample. In later chapters we will look at how individual teachers, schools and local authorities have responded to these developments and how, in practical terms, CPD is impacting practice.

Radical change – or the emperor's new clothes?

Before we can come to an informed conclusion about the benefits which might accrue from CPD, it is important to clarify the term itself. To that end, it is necessary to take each element in turn, before asking if the whole is more than the sum of the individual parts.

Continuing

Our good doctor, used as a touchstone at the beginning of this chapter, had managed to 'escape' from CPD. Now, teachers who entered the profession from 2003 onwards, and those, more experienced colleagues already in post can look forward to a process of professional development. 'Standards' have now been developed in teaching from initial teacher education through to headship. The Standards in Scotland's Schools etc. Act of 2000 introduced the term 'career development' and made statutory provision for the General Teaching Council for Scotland (GTCS) to have national responsibility in this area. The first set of competences for newly qualified teachers was issued in 1993 in *Conditions for Teacher Training Courses*. They were introduced in 1998, with revised guidelines, setting out some 24 'benchmarks', each beginning with the phrase 'the programme of initial teacher education will enable students to...'.

The Standard for Full Registration emerged in 2001 after a review of the probationary period carried out by GTC(S) and was designed to be compatible with the Initial Teacher Education (ITE) standard. Then, in the wake of the McCrone Agreement, Standards for Continuing Professional Development formed part of the emerging CPD 'framework'. As part of the Scottish Qualification for Headship (SQH), a set of competences was devised and a framework for professional development set out (Lennon 2003) which emphasised values. Finally, to complete the set, the Standard for Chartered Teacher was published in 2002. In all of these publications, there is a consistency of language which suggests an attempt to ensure that from ITE to retirement, teachers, in classrooms and in management, will be expected to engage in CPD.

Professional

What does the term 'professional' mean and can teachers claim to be professionals in the same way that our doctor and his colleagues, along with lawyers and others, can? Is professionalism absolute, something which you have or don't have or can it be seen rather as a continuum, with some having more professionality (Hoyle 1974) than others?

McBer (2001: p. 202) outlines 'professional characteristics', defined as 'deep-seated patterns of behaviour which outstanding teachers display more often, in more circumstances and to a greater degree of intensity than effective colleagues'. The model of professional characteristics advanced includes five 'clusters', professionalism, thinking, planning and setting expectations, leading and relating to others, but within professionalism the key elements are:

> **Respect for others:** the underlying belief that individuals matter.
> **Challenge and support:** commitment to enable all pupils to be successful.
> **Confidence:** belief in one's ability to take on challenges.
> **Creating trust:** being consistent and keeping one's word.

Munro (2001) suggests that 'it is reasonable to expect a strong nexus between teacher effectiveness and school effectiveness.' He cites Scheerens and Bosker (1997) who support the view that 'teacher knowledge about learning may influence the effectiveness of a school.' Munro's own research, involving 32 teachers in Melbourne schools, traced the teachers' 'effective learning behaviours' after a programme of staff development and found, interestingly, that variables such as age, gender, level of qualifications or experience did not appear to correlate with success. He concludes that there can be a positive link between professional development programmes and teacher behaviour in classrooms and argues that this is more likely to happen when the teachers are able to develop their own explicit theories of learning.

Thus, the imperative for professional development seems to revolve around making teachers more reflective about their own theories and practice, improving their performance in the classroom and so contributing to school improvement. At the same time, schools are seen as collectives, where teachers, and others, work together, and have a moral obligation to share good practice, (Fullan 2001) and where high expectations of all pupils is the aim.

Development

The word 'development' has been around in this context for some time. Does it simply imply 'change' or is there a sense in which 'improvement' is assumed? Certainly, not all teachers in the past would have agreed with Munro's conclusions above. For them, development was something done *to* them, at someone else's behest, with little follow up to ascertain whether anything had changed in the classroom as a result. Fullan (2001: p. 76) has argued that 'change is needed because many teachers are frustrated, bored and burnt out' and suggests that 'if teaching becomes neither terribly interesting nor exciting to many teachers can one expect them to make learning interesting and exciting to students?'

This definition of development as change links the personal job satisfaction of teachers with the effectiveness of pupil learning. Fullan stresses the collective nature of schools but is at pains to point out that consensus and conformity is not the aim of professional development. He stresses the need to preserve the individuality of teachers and suggest that an effective school would have a 'network of people working on similar problems'. His suggestion that 'multiple focused collaborative networks' enable schools to make the most of the talents of individual teachers, is a challenging one in an age where headteachers are encouraged to try to focus all staff on a small number of 'whole-school' issues.

The real challenge facing those who want teachers to continue to develop their professionalism throughout their careers is to ensure that the programmes offered to teachers do not stifle their creativity, do not force them into an ideological conformity and do not restrict their abilities to contribute to the effectiveness of the schools in which they work. An American visitor once asked the present author, when he was the head of a secondary school, why it was that he didn't personally select all of his staff, presumably in order to surround himself with like-minded people. It is an attractive proposition, but essentially false, since the strength of any school lies in its diversity, in the range of talents and experiences the staff bring with them and in the variety of teaching approaches they use. The challenge for the headteacher is surely to enable these qualities to interact and to ensure that the whole is more than the sum of the individual parts?

CPD – *1984* or *Brave New World*?

Orwell's apocalyptic vision recognised the importance of language and its impact on thought. The thought police were a part of the State's apparatus of control and some would see CPD as one strand in the Scottish Executive's strategy to create a new breed of teacher. CPD can be seen, if you subscribe to the conspiracy theory, as an agent of control. It is less an entitlement than a requirement. Will failure to maintain an up-to-date portfolio be a bar to promotion within the profession? Could it be linked, in the future, to performance-related pay? Is it a way of 'encouraging' teachers to read more, do research and visit one another's classrooms?

Some commentators are critical of the staff development ideology spawned by Michael Forsyth and taken up with gusto by the Audit Unit of Her Majesty's Inspectorate. They are critical, too, of terms like 'reflective practitioner' which seek to de-skill and de-professionalise teachers. In an environment where there were Performance Indicators, written by HMI and used by them to rate schools and teachers (using a four-point scale), where targets for examination pass rates for each school in Scotland are set nationally and where staff development and review are being imposed, it is difficult to see CPD as liberating or empowering. It seems to be about control and about compliance. Hartley and Roger (1990) observe that in Scotland, educational policy-making was once characterised by 'debate followed by consensus'. By publishing the original paper *Curriculum and Assessment: a Policy for the 90s* in 1987, without any prior discussion even within the Inspectorate, Michael Forsyth the then Conservative Education Minister heralded a move to 'consultation followed by imposition'.

Thus, even when a change which appears to be benign in its intention, is proposed, there is a sense in which the Scottish teaching profession remains sceptical.

CPD – best value for all?

So, does the term CPD herald a new dawn in Scottish education or is it about control? Is the entitlement of 35 hours of CPD per year for all teachers any more than a thinly disguised attempt to ensure that teachers conform to whatever orthodoxy is current at any given moment? Already, in 2004, change is beginning to take place. Not only has CPD become the umbrella term for all activities previously described as in-service training or staff development, with the addition of some activities which tended to be the preserve only of a few teachers, but schools and local authorities are gearing up for change.

Certification is a new development. The probationary period for teachers has changed from two years to one, and there is a national agreement that it will take place in one school, not the piecemeal approach of 'supply' teaching in various schools which was often the case before. In addition, probationary teachers can expect 0.3 of their week (i.e. 30 per cent of the week or 1.5 days) to be set aside for CPD, and many Local Authorities are providing a range of quality experiences for them, many of which will lead to a postgraduate module. Menmure (2003) describes how, nationally, these individual modules can be accumulated to enable teachers to achieve a Certificate (four Modules), a Diploma, (eight Modules) and a Masters degree (twelve Modules). In the case of the new post of Chartered Teacher, substantial increases in salary accompany these achievements, and even where teachers are undertaking these activities purely for their own personal development, it is likely they will want some kind of certification to include in their (now compulsory) CPD Portfolio.

CPD – winning hearts and minds

The traditional scepticism of teachers towards in-service training activities is unlikely to change overnight simply by giving it a new name. CPD will stand or fall on the basis of its quality, credibility and relevance to the professional aspirations of teachers. Undoubtedly, it is linked to the school improvement agenda, and few teachers will quibble with that. If change is indeed the only constant in education, then teachers deserve to be given the means to make it work.

It has been argued that the Government may have a view of the change process which is cynical and manipulative. Michael Barber, senior New Labour adviser, adapting Pascale's seventeenth century argument about prayer, suggested that:

> Sometimes it is necessary to mandate the change, implement it well, consciously change the prevailing culture, and then have the courage to sustain it until beliefs shift.

He argues that 'winning hearts and minds is not the best first step in any *urgent* [my emphasis] process of change'. Pascale had argued that the best way to get people to pray was to get down on your knees first, and the prayer would follow. Here is a Government adviser essentially arguing that in education, change was simply a case of getting the body along and the mind would follow!

The dilemma here is that CPD presupposes that teachers are capable of being reflective, that change should be the result of a process of 'argument, consultation, debate, dialogue' and that individuals will be more committed to organisational goals if they have played a part in shaping them.

Fullan (1995: p. 253) has argued that; 'Professional development of teachers has a poor track record because it lacks a theoretical base and coherent focus.' While many teachers might cite other reasons for having a poor opinion of professional development activities, there is no doubt that much of it in the past has been seen as *ad hoc*, policy-driven and ideologically biased. Adey *et al.* (2004) offers three kinds of theory which might underpin professional development, namely general notions of how change takes place, the idea of the reflective professional and the concept of teachers' intuitive knowledge, and suggests that CPD should explicitly examine the inter-relatedness of these theories as they attempt to explain the learning and teaching process.

The current view is that a teaching force which becomes used to high quality CPD, from entry to exit, so to speak, is also one which will be more capable of being more reflective (Schon 1987) and of questioning policy. There is a risk for government in creating a well-read, reflective and empowered profession. As teachers become aware of the theories underpinning learning, as their understanding of the change process grows and as they become more used to engaging in critical evaluation, they may also be less likely to accept Barber's paradigm of change.

The professional development of teachers – theory and practice

Adey *et al.* (2004: p. 143) suggest that since 'the nature of professional development for teachers relates directly to the nature of teaching', the notions which underpin teacher education at any one time reflect the dominant view of what teaching is. They cite the age-old debate as to whether teaching is an art or a science and suggest that ideas such as theory-driven action, simple apprenticeship, the unguided reflective practitioner and craft-skill to scholastic rationality, all stem from belief systems along the art–science continuum. At one end of the continuum is the notion that teaching is too complex to be susceptible to training or regulation by competences to the opposite technical–rational view that teaching is a set of skills based on sound theory and supported by well-tested methods. Stoll and Fink (1996) have echoed Hartley's concern about the idea of teacher as quasi-professional ('practitioner') and have suggested that it is based on a narrow 'transmission sequential notion of knowledge'.

Adey *et al.* have pointed out that there are pitfalls in all of the above positions and support the view that:

> 'The postmodernist relativist interpretation of learning as a reflective practitioner [sic] falls into a trap similar to that of the old apprenticeship model, by underrepresenting what is known about teaching and placing too much reliance on the subjective truths of the individual without reference to external evaluation.'
>
> (2004: p. 144)

Adey *et al.* make the counter-balancing point that too much reliance on an 'evidence-based' approach 'may place too much faith on the reliability of objective truth' (2004: p. 144).

The 'activist' teaching profession

In their foreword to Sachs' *The Activist Teaching Profession* (2003), Hargreaves and Goodson assert that 'teaching today is increasingly complex work, requiring the highest standards of professional practice to perform it well' (2003: p. ix). They claim that teachers are the 'midwives of [that] knowledge society'. At the same time as George Bush is using the slogan 'leave no child behind', the teaching profession is 'in crisis' because of the demographic exodus of the baby boomers. Across the developed world, teacher recruitment is struggling to keep up with demand while at the same time governments are placing more and more hope in the transformational power of education. In England and Wales, *Excellence and Enjoyment* (2003) has heralded 'new and planned freedoms' for (primary) teachers while in Scotland the Ministerial Review Group on the Curriculum 3–18 is looking at what the 1947 Advisory Council on the (secondary) Curriculum called 'ordered freedom'. They suggest that Sachs' notion of 'the activist teaching profession' is timely because of the debate about old and new professionalism. In her 'futurist analysis', Sachs looks at the moral and social visions which underpin teaching.

Sachs argues that to create an activist profession there needs to be a new set of relationships between teacher educators and the profession. She suggests six important roles:

Advising
Teacher educators have expertise in terms of approaches to research, policy-making and practice. They can also influence the system by reconceptualising teacher education programmes.

Issue and problem identification
Teacher educators can carry out research *with* teachers, creating a debate on the one hand and offering solutions to problems on the other.

Spreading ideas
Ideas need to be spread and disseminated and they need champions and advocates. Teacher educators, in their work with emerging teachers and within the policy community at large, can help spread ideas.

Providing alternative perspectives
Acting individually or with other stakeholders, teacher educators can present various possibilities without risk of being dismissed out of hand. They can exert the kind of influence which governments may wish to use.

Evaluating programmes
Independent evaluation is a key function of teacher educators. It may be fraught with tensions in terms of the aspirations of funders and the need for evaluators to remain objective, but it can sometimes result in alternative models being offered.

Advocacy

Advocacy may be of ideas or of groups within the system. It often involves strategic thinking and planning as well as excellent communication.

For Sachs, the time has come for teacher educators to 'take intellectual and moral leadership' (2003: p. 76). In Scotland, Initial Teacher Education is under review but it is arguable whether the notions of professionalism proposed by Sachs will feature in the deliberation of the review group. Instead, as Kirk (2003) has suggested, the Second Stage Review will consider another 'agenda for change', including:

- Part-time provision.
- The relationship between ITE and in-service provision, particularly in view of the abbreviated form of probation and the introduction of the Standard for Chartered Teacher.
- The need for a teaching qualification which straddles primary and secondary education in response to such developments as the 5–14 programme.
- The need for a teaching qualification which straddles upper secondary and further education in response to the Higher Still programme.
- Greater opportunities for specialised study within the B.Ed. (primary).
- Introduction of a teaching qualification in personal, social or lifestyle education in response to Scotland's appalling record in health and related matters.
- Further developments of concurrent approaches.
  (2003: p. 930)

SUMMARY

In recent years, there has emerged a growing realisation that continuing professional development can no longer be optional for teachers if 'continuing improvement' is to be achieved in education. CPD in the twenty-first century is more than a rehash of what was 'in-service training', and the McCrone Agreement has made it an entitlement for all staff. The range of activities which are now accepted as CPD has widened, too, including reading, research, shared classroom observation and participation in working groups. Career-long CPD will become the norm and it should contribute in a positive way to a new professionalism among teachers. Research has indicated that CPD is at the heart of school improvement and collaborative models have emerged as key to the successful management of change. In the past, in-service training was often 'done to' teachers. Now a body of research and theory has been developed which locates CPD at the heart of the improvement agenda. Sachs (2003) has argued that the teaching profession must adapt and become more 'activist', and challenges teacher educators to engage in new ways with the profession.

POINTS FOR REFLECTION

1 To what extent is CPD an 'entitlement' rather than a compulsory, contractual obligation for teachers?

2 Is the range of CPD activities offered by the Scottish Executive realistic and can schools and Local Authorities offer opportunities for teachers to engage in all of these?

3 Is the traditional balance of CPD, with most of it taking place outside the school in the form of courses, likely to shift, and if so, in what ways?

4 How will we judge whether CPD is making an impact on teacher and school improvement?

2 A brief history of CPD

> So they went. At first Pooh and Rabbit and Piglet
> walked together, and Tigger ran round them in
> circles, and then, when the path got narrower,
> Rabbit, Piglet and Pooh walked one after
> another, and Tigger ran round them in oblongs,
> and bye-and-bye, when the gorse got very prickly
> on each side of the path, Tigger ran up and down
> in front of them, and sometimes he bounced
> into Rabbit and sometimes he didn't.
>
> *The House at Pooh Corner*, **A. A. Milne**

From pre-service to in-service training

While the term CPD may be of relatively recent origin, the
concept of training for teachers while they are in service (as
opposed to pre-service) is not new. Over the last 100 years or so,
the nature of the training, the range of providers and the sources
of funding have certainly changed, but has the quality and
relevance of the training improved in that time? Indeed, how
would we know? Is there a body of research or evaluation which
has taken place over that time which can inform present-day
discussions about CPD? For many teachers, in-service training
often seemed haphazard and unplanned. Just as Tigger seemed to
get in the way of Pooh, Rabbit and Piglet, in-service training
often seemed to interfere with the process of teaching, and many
of the so-called new ideas did not seem to be helpful in the
classroom.

In their book *Teaching the Teachers* (1996: p. 1), Harrison
and Marker remind us that:

> When, in 1894, Glasgow University introduced its first MA
> course in education, listed among the set books was *The training*

system of education by David Stow. On the face of it, this is quite astonishing. By then the original book was more than 60 years old; even the 11th edition, published in 1859, must have seemed out of date to end-of-the-century students.

Teacher training had begun in the late 1820s and it was Stow who established the principle that teachers should be trained. It was almost a century later that teacher training institutions became involved in in-service as well as pre-service training (Mortimer 1996: p. 122).

'Further instruction of teachers in actual service' had been previously the responsibility of the County Councils but in 1906, it passed to the training colleges. School Boards and County Councils could make requests and the colleges would set fees and establish minimum numbers. The Scottish Education Department (SED) retained rights of 'approval, inspection and certification' and thus in-service training was kept under close central control. Mortimer observes (1996: p. 122) County Councils from across Scotland made requests to Jordanhill College, often asking for classes to be run locally and by local staff. This pattern continued for many years, long after the National Committee for the Training of Teachers (NCTT) took over the teacher training colleges.

For many years, classes were held during evenings and Saturdays primarily aimed at those teachers wishing to enhance their qualifications. While some of these classes were held during vacations, so too were courses which did not form part of an award. Thus the distinction between award-bearing and non award-bearing was born and continued well into the latter part of the twentieth century. The latter, over the years, included the Infant Mistress qualification, various Additional Teaching Qualifications, an MD course (for those teaching mentally defective children), and, later in the twentieth century, modern methods in the primary school, speech training and Guidance (Mortimer 1996: p. 125).

In the 1950s, the balance began to shift, and non award-bearing courses began to grow in popularity. Mortimer suggests that this was due in part to changes in national curriculum and examinations structures, and suggests that the fact that staff from Jordanhill, and other colleges, were often on national working groups and, therefore, in the forefront of developments, meant that courses run by college staff were held in high esteem.

By the 1970s, Jordanhill was mounting up to fifteen national subject conferences per year, enabling teachers to meet and hear about the latest developments in their field. In the mid-1960s, Jordanhill had decided to form a dedicated team of tutors in an In-Service Department. For some twenty years, the department would be at the forefront of developments, particularly in primary education. The publication in 1965 of *The Primary Memorandum* had introduced potentially far-reaching changes in philosophy and methodology, and the team of staff tutors (as they came to be called) developed approaches to topic work which revolutionised primary education in Scotland and, eventually, in many countries across the world.

In 1967, a National Committee for the In-service Training of Teachers (NCITT) was established, to be replaced some twenty years later by the Scottish Committee for Staff Development in Education (SCOSDE). The Colleges continued to play a key role, with in-service training suites being created and courses being aimed at senior managers as well as classroom teachers. Meanwhile, local government re-organisation had created the largest education authority ever seen in Scotland, and Strathclyde began to have an important influence on the kind of in-service training which Jordanhill, and other colleges, would deliver. Strathclyde also built up a formidable team of advisers, capable of organising and delivering in-service training of a high quality. The colleges had to respond quickly, especially when SED, in response to the easing of teacher shortages, shifted significant sections of the budget from pre-service to school-focused in-service training.

Alongside the colleges, Her Majesty's Inspectorate of Education (HMI) had been prime movers, and shakers, in curricular innovation and development. In 1977, three major national committees reported on the structure and balance of the curriculum in S3 and S4 (*Munn*), certification and assessment in S3 and S4 (*Dunning*) and truancy and indiscipline in Scottish schools (*Pack*). The first two of these had implications for the exam system and for the structure of the curriculum in secondary schools and so had to be implemented immediately. The third was concerned with the nature of schooling, the aims of education, the relevance of the curriculum for all learners and equality of opportunity, and so was less easy to turn into direct action. Nevertheless, HMI set about ensuring that *Munn* and *Dunning* would change forever the face of the secondary school and the examination system. A national 'Feasibility Study' was carried out into the Foundation Level of the new award system. Conferences were organised, good practice was shared and staff development was at the heart of the initiative. Meanwhile, a national structure for the development of teaching materials was created with advisers throughout the country taking the leading role and, financed from the centre, managing groups of their colleagues to ensure that teachers in schools had teaching materials to support the new system. National and Local Authority co-operation on such a scale had never happened before, and would never happen again. For some, the creation of centrally-produced materials was the hallmark of the success of the Standard Grade (as it came to be known) development; for others, it was the beginning of the end of teacher autonomy and trust and the beginning of central control of the curriculum.

Perhaps the biggest changes to the pattern of in-service provision came in the mid-1980s and early 1990s when SED changed the nature of funding for in-service training. First, it introduced specific grant funding for in-service training which addressed national priorities and demanded that Local Authorities and colleges establish contracts for the provision of such training. Thus, the centre began to exert more control over the content and focus of in-service training. This was strengthened in 1991 when the funding was given directly to the Local Authorities. Secondly, it recognised that there could be a range of providers, including a burgeoning private sector. Joining the traditional providers – the colleges of education (now fast being incorporated into University Faculties of Education), local authority advisory services and Her Majesty's Inspectorate of Education – were independent providers, sometimes from south of the border in England and Wales where the education system was embracing 'privatisation' under successive Conservative governments. Increasingly, the independent providers were Scottish, often former Local Authority personnel or people who had worked in central organisations such as the Scottish Council for Educational Technology.

Finally, in keeping with what was happening in England and Wales, the money for CPD was devolved to schools themselves. Notwithstanding the fact that local authorities in Scotland continued to 'top-slice' budgets earmarked for CPD, the balance of power has shifted irrevocably. 'He-who-pays-the-piper-calls-the-tune' became the prevailing philosophy. Never again could colleges of education simply send any member of staff who was available to conduct in-service training. The organisation paying the bill could now specify not only the nature of the course to be delivered, but even the person who should deliver it. Evaluations now became *de rigueur* after every in-service course, and poor evaluations from participants would ensure that the course would not be repeated. In 1974, after local government re-organisation, Strathclyde – the largest Local Authority in the country, covering half of Scotland's population – was created, and a new player with irresistible clout entered the scene.

Strathclyde Regional Council – monstrosity or innovator?

Strathclyde consisted of six 'divisions – Glasgow, Lanarkshire, Renfrewshire, Ayrshire, Dunbartonshire and Argyll and Bute. It had a single Director of Education, six Divisional Education Officers, and, importantly, six advisory services, with individuals who had responsibility for primary education generally, and, in most cases, with advisers for every subject in the secondary curriculum. This was an imposing cadre of people, many of whom had national reputations in their field, who served on national subject panels of the Scottish Examination Board, on Central Committees for individual subjects as well as for primary education and on subject groups for Munn and Dunning developments. Other regions in Scotland – there were thirteen in all – had their advisory services and their national figures, but Strathclyde had a critical mass. Not only that but politically, the region was Socialist (thus earning it the immortal epithet, 'monstrosity' from the lips of John Major, the successor to Mrs Thatcher) and, consequently, throughout the 1980s and 1990s, almost constantly in opposition to government policy. Quite simply, Strathclyde had the muscle to go it alone if it wanted to and it had the capacity to provide all of the CPD it needed, in-house, if it wanted to. Not only that, Strathclyde was pioneering Devolved Management of Resources (DMR) in Scotland, and money was going directly to schools.

By 1990, Strathclyde had had its first major change of regime within the education department. The resultant shake-up saw the appointment of a new director, the establishment of a Quality Assurance structure (the first time a local authority Inspectorate had ever been established in Scotland), a regional layer for the hitherto divisional advisory service and the appointment of a Head of Staff College, signalling the intention to place CPD at the heart of educational improvement in the region.

While all of this was taking place, the SED was allowing colleges of education to run any course which was self-financing, as had already happened in England and Wales. Mortimer has described such courses as 'full-cost entrepreneurial venture(s)'. Such courses could lead to qualifications at Certificate, Diploma and Masters level, through a series of modular courses, and individuals could get accreditation for prior learning. At its height, some 2000 students, mostly teachers and social workers, were enrolled in such courses in Jordanhill alone.

While on many issues Strathclyde and the Scottish Office Education Department (SOED) were at odds, the old adage that Scottish education was 'centrally governed and locally administered' was still partly true. Local authorities as large and powerful as Strathclyde did more than merely 'administer' education. They had their own Education Committees made up of elected representatives, their own directorates of education and their own advisory services. They could make and implement policy, and did so, innovatively, in many cases. Lothian Region established its own model of community schools in the 1970s; Grampian pioneered an area model of support for learning in the 1980s; Strathclyde instituted its own approach to pre-5 education, introduced its adults-in-schools initiative and set up Area Curriculum Planning Groups in the 1980s, and, as has been indicated before, formed its own Inspectorate in the 1990s. However, the adage did imply a kind of partnership between the centre and the local authorities, and this remained the case throughout the 1980s and 1990s. Local Authority personnel served on national groups, including those which planned the CPD arrangements to support the national 5–14 programme, the Higher Still (Opportunity for All) programme as well as new initiatives on special educational needs, able pupils, school development planning and Management Training for Head Teachers (MTHT), to name but a few.

Nevertheless, the balance of power was shifting. In the early 1990s, Strathclyde's Head of Staff College, while having none of the traditional background of enmity between the authority and the SOED (having been appointed from England, itself a sign that things were changing since Strathclyde had a reputation for 'appointing its own'), quickly set about harnessing the talent within the advisory service and among senior staff in schools and began not by opposing the SOED's initiatives but by improving on them. The MTHT programme had been widely criticised. The production of the nine Modules which every headteacher was going to have to undertake, had been rushed and disjointed. SOEID (by now it was the Scottish Office Education *and Industry* Department) had poured lots of money into the commissioning of the Modules but had failed to engage experienced headteachers sufficiently in the process. The result was Modules which often seemed content-free and which, in the early days, were led by tutors inexperienced in the management of schools. The Strathclyde Staff College was able to second senior staff from schools to work alongside advisers and others from Colleges of Education and elsewhere, to re-write the Modules. Not only that, the budget for staff development in Strathclyde could be used to ensure that coverage of existing headteachers was achieved; economies of scale could be made and headteachers could be released from schools to attend residential courses in comfortable hotels, and the messages about leadership and good management would be those with which the authority was happy.

In the meantime, advisers continued to meet in their national subject groupings and found themselves represented on every 5–14 curricular group. They helped develop the framework for the various curricular areas and they participated in the planning of the staff development which accompanied the Guidelines. Here, too, local authorities took the lead. In order to facilitate curricular change, and partly to avoid the stand off which took place in the industrial action of the mid-1980s, SOEID had granted every school five in-service days when pupils were not present and which should be used for CPD. In addition, many of the local authorities top-sliced the specific grant budget for particular aspects of the curriculum (for example, 5–14, Higher Still, SEN) and mounted their own in-service training. At around this time, schools had become familiar with School Development Planning, various approaches to Devolved Management and, increasingly, what became known as the Quality Process, in other words, using a range of self-evaluation tools, from the National Performance and Ethos Indicators to local authority devised Quality Pointers. Schools were becoming adept at planning their own staff development, often appointing senior staff with a CPD remit and involving advisers, college of education staff or external consultants in the delivery of the in-service training.

Larger Authorities, like Strathclyde, mounted their own conferences on a regular basis on aspects of curriculum development, while smaller authorities joined forces to do so. Indeed, it was fast becoming an expectation that no significant change should take place without staff development.

Local government re-organisation – fragmentation and regrouping

In 1996, a second major re-organisation of local government took place in Scotland, barely twenty years after the first. Out of thirteen Local Authorities, there sprang 32; out of Strathclyde alone, there emerged twelve – each with its own director of education and all of them with the remnants of previous advisory services. At the same time, most of the colleges of education had merged with universities or were contemplating doing so. The momentum built up prior to re-organisation was lost and many of the new Councils turned their backs on all things 'regional'. Predictably, Strathclyde attracted the greatest opprobrium. As we will see in Chapter 3, its top-down, authoritarian model of management – of all things, including CPD – ensured that structures which had existed previously were rejected by the new Councils. Many had advisory services which were too small to provide the CPD required by the schools. Others wanted to turn their advisers into 'adspectors' in their quest for quality assurance. Some were big enough to go it alone; others had to forge new relationships with the new Faculties of Education.

For a time it seemed that HMI would fill the void. The Audit Unit, a creation of the Conservative Education Minister, Michael Forsyth, was proactive in commissioning work from Faculties of Education to support their views on Homework, Truancy, School Self-Evaluation, Study Support and School Development Planning. They poured money into conferences, research and new technology such as CDIs and CD-ROMs with no commitment to any evaluation of their impact. They set up national networks on 'ethos', 'able pupils' and 'learning and teaching' which did stand the test of time and still make a significant contribution to CPD nationally. They were involved in both making policy and in assessing those who carried it out. It was only a matter of time before the profession objected.

Most importantly, the new Councils were beginning to find their own identities and they quickly realised that a commitment to CPD was at the heart of their desire to improve educational achievement and tackle social exclusion. As HMI became an 'agency', detached from policy-making, it was the Councils which took the lead. The final change to take place in the twentieth century was a new agreement among government, councils and teachers' unions on pay and conditions of service. *A Teaching Profession for the 21st Century* (known as the McCrone Agreement, after the chair of the committee) was set to change CPD in Scotland for ever.

A teaching profession for the twenty-first century

In her chapter 'The Professional Development of Teachers' in the second, post-devolution edition of *Scottish Education (2003)*, Aileen Purdon suggests that 'improved opportunities for career-long professional development were to be seen as part of a package of measures designed to enhance the teaching profession' (2003: p. 943). The notional CPD framework which emerged from *A Teaching Profession for the 21st Century* is, in Purdon's view, problematic since the various components may not, in fact, add up to a coherent framework. In 1999, a Ministerial strategy committee was established to steer the development and implementation of this framework. The elements of the framework include benchmarks for Initial Teacher Education, a new Standard for Full Registration of teachers, the Chartered Teacher Programme, and, it could be argued, Scottish Qualification for Headship. Thus, theoretically, CPD of a high quality and leading to qualifications, in many cases at postgraduate level, was to be available throughout the career of a teacher. Purdon points to the fact that in some cases the individual elements of this 'new' framework already existed and suggests that the different processes for arriving at these standards (in some cases in-house, by the GTCS; in others put out to tender to public-private partnerships) indicates a level of pragmatism in the development of the framework.

As we will see in Chapter 6, the Chartered Teacher programme is now well underway, but it was not without controversy when the concept was introduced. Its antecedents were not propitious. The ill-fated attempt in the 1990s to reward good, experienced classroom teachers gave rise to the post of Senior Teacher. The original intention was to provide an alternative method of rewarding such teachers rather than the 'managerial' route through traditional promoted posts. However, once the dust had settled on the negotiations between the teaching unions and the management side, Senior Teacher had become another step on the promotion ladder. Not only was the term 'experienced' problematic and so was gradually dropped, but the duties attached to some Senior Teacher posts bordered on the ludicrous. Indeed, in some small primary schools with only the headteacher having a managerial role, the Senior Teacher's remit seemed indistinguishable from that of an Assistant Headteacher in a larger school. Meanwhile, in large secondary schools, the Senior Teacher's remit could be very narrowly defined.

For many headteachers, the concept of the Chartered Teacher is highly problematic. For the first time in recent history, the headteacher, by national agreement, has no locus in the process of deciding which of her/his staff can embark on the Chartered Teacher course, how it is funded, the nature of the work being done in school which forms part of the assessment or, most controversially, how the qualified Chartered Teacher will use her/his newly acquired knowledge and skills within the establishment. While in reality, where the climate and culture of the establishments is collegial and supportive, all of these issues may well be discussed in a professional way, in others, the Chartered Teacher may simply see the process as a personal one, with no obligation than to become a more effective classroom teacher.

However, the management route remains open to teachers and the Ministerial group established the Leadership and Management Pathways (LAMPS) sub-group. Taking this route is less certain for teachers since it carries no promise of automatic salary increase as Modules are completed. Somewhat illogically, the Chartered Teacher programme leads to a Masters level qualification, while the Scottish Qualification for Headship is at the lower Diploma level. However, while these issues are of interest to close observers of the educational policy-making process, it is the ongoing, career-long CPD implications of the McCrone report which might, arguably, have the greatest impact on Scottish education. There is no doubt that CPD which is provided by local authorities and by mainstream providers such as University Faculties of Education, will be heavily influenced by national and local priorities. The offerings of the Universities will, no doubt be along the lines of the Strathclyde catalogue entitled *Professional Development Unit: Catalogue of Providers* (2004). It promotes itself by saying:

> The Faculty of Education has a long and distinguished history in teacher education and in the training of professionals in the arts, community education, physical education, sport and outdoor education, social work and speech and language therapy. Its profile is being continually enhanced by the research and consultancy activities of its academic staff.

The Faculty offers a wide range of undergraduate and postgraduate courses which aim to:

- Address a wide range of issues and concerns to practitioners in the professions served by the Faculty.
- Provide the opportunity for institutions and individuals to build on existing knowledge and skills.
- Extend understanding of professional techniques, competences and professional issues.
- Enhance confidence.

(2004: p. 3)

The Professional Development Unit itself has a mission statement 'to provide a high quality service to the academic staff in the faculty and to our clients in the professions' and lists its key activities as:

- Stimulating and supporting short courses and conferences.
- Managing and administering major award bearing courses including the Chartered Teacher Programme, the Scottish Qualification for Headship, Advanced Professional Studies and the Management and Leadership in Education Programme within the Modular Masters Scheme.
- Establishing and maintaining partnerships with our professional colleagues in the UK and internationally.

(2004: p. 3)

Thus, a major provider sets out its stall, conscious of the changing landscape, perhaps a little self-consciously adopting the language of the market-place ('clients'), promoting the skills of its staff (the folder contains some 40 pages of pen-pictures of staff with their particular professional interests) and making connections with the main elements in the national CPD agenda.

However, not withstanding the range and quality of such offerings, from established providers and from an increasing number of consultants and commercial organisations in the field of CPD, it may be that the legacy of McCrone will be a shift in the balance of external and internal provision of CPD. Fullan has argued that schools which wish to improve as organisations should make greater use of the talent and expertise within their own organisation. Given that the 'cluster' – secondary and associated schools – may be emerging as the unit for management and curriculum planning purposes, then the possibilities of teachers sharing insights and examples of good practice within a CPD forum may become increasingly important and increasingly feasible. Thus, the teachers' entitlement of 35 hours CPD per year, with the wide range of activities including reading and research as well as shared observation of lessons, may be a more important catalyst for change than the Standards or the new pathways to advancement.

Towards an National Strategy for Scotland

In 2004, the Scottish Executive Education Department (SEED) appointed Margaret Alcorn, formerly head of CPD in Edinburgh City Council, to the newly created post of National Co-ordinator for CPD. With a remit to 'encourage best practice', and already dubbed the 'CPD Tsar', she will work within the structure provided by the 'four pillars' of:

- Intial teacher education.
- Standard for full registration.
- Chartered teacher status.
- Standard for headship.

Her main concern at the outset is that all 32 local authorities in Scotland are re-inventing the wheel and that they should be working more closely together. A budget of a third of a million pounds for each of the two years of the project and the capacity to second staff for specific initiatives suggests that this post is being given some scope to be creative and flexible. She is physically located within COSLA headquarters in Edinburgh, not within

SEED, sending a signal that it is local authorities in partnership with universities, the General Teaching Council (Scotland), Learning and Teaching Scotland, teaching unions and other providers who will take the lead in CPD.

Her comments to the *Times Educational Supplement Scotland* (May 2004) suggest that she sees CPD as having the potential to 'energise' the teaching profession. It should give a 'buzz' to the professional practice and to the thinking of teachers, and should produce, in the medium term, a profession of 'reflective practitioners'. However, in a little editorial aside, the writer of the *TESS* article suggests that there may still be a tension between CPD which benefits the authorities and that which benefits teachers. Is the goal effectiveness or efficiency, or both?

Her stated goal is a 'Scotland-wide approach to CPD', more integrated and consistent. The fact that education authorities are 're-inventing the wheel' is seen as a problem and her task is to encourage more collaborative approaches. Her sentiments are echoed by Professor Douglas Weir who is quoted in the same article as saying that:

> There has been less of a culture of collegiality in our schools that might be desired. Hopefully, the flatter structures of school management and the chartered teacher programme will address this.
>
> (TESS May 2004)

He goes on to float the notion that 'every teacher needs a mentor, not just the probationer teacher', opening up a debate about the role of the teacher as reflective professional and suggesting, by implication, that teachers are learners too and that their learning is best done with colleagues in their own establishments with support from Faculty of Education and local authority staff working in partnership.

CPD may yet turn out to be a Pandora's box. Once the profession becomes more confident and better informed, it may be less compliant and more proactive in pursuit of what it believes is in the best interest of education. Activism may not have been the goal of the McCrone Committee, but it may be one of the unintended consequences of an increased engagement with new ideas and intellectually and professionally challenging CPD.

SUMMARY

In-service training grew historically from the pre-service work done in colleges of education. In-service departments grew up in the colleges and a range of award-bearing courses grew up aimed at experienced teachers. Local authority advisers were heavily involved in in-service training and for periods of time HMI took leading roles in national training to support curriculum change. Gradually, the funding for in-service training was transferred to local authorities and then to schools. Strathclyde region, the largest in Scotland, had enough critical mass to develop its own brand of in-service training and for a short period had a Staff College which, while it had no physical location, was successful in mounting high quality training for heads and others. The McCrone report has now established CPD as the key element in the improvement agenda, establishing the Chartered Teacher post as a non-management route to professional advancement for teachers. Universities individually and in partnerships have responded by providing the postgraduate training to support the CT programme. To create a national strategy for CPD, a 'tzar' has been appointed with a brief to co-ordinate good practice.

POINTS FOR REFLECTION

1. Have the changes which have taken place in in-service training over the years all been positive?

2. What is your view of the Feasibility Study approach to the introduction of new initiatives?

3. What should be the role of the local authority in terms of CPD?

4. If you were appointed to develop CPD nationally, what would be your priorities?

5. What should be the contribution of HMIE?

3 CPD – the 'Postman Pat' model

> And then he thought that being with Christopher
> Robin was a very good thing to do, and having
> Piglet near was a very friendly thing to have; and
> so, when he had thought it all out, he said,
> 'What I like best in the whole world is Me and
> Piglet going to see You, and You saying, 'What
> about a little something?' and Me saying, 'Well,
> I shouldn't mind a little something, should you,
> Piglet?', and it being a hummy sort of day
> outside, and birds singing.'
> *The House at Pooh Corner*, A. A. Milne

It's all about relationships

Professional Development is all about relationships. The decision-making process, the extent of the involvement of the participants, the setting of the agenda and the ownership which people have of the process, are all crucial to the quality of the experience. How many people who have gone, or perhaps have been sent, on courses have come back thinking that it had been a 'hummy sort of day'? How many have been asked 'What about a little something?' instead of being consulted or being asked to negotiate the learning outcomes? How many of the tutors or leaders of CPD courses have made the experience one in which participants felt their needs were being met? In other words, where are decisions made about the needs of those who are engaging in CPD activities?

The 'Postman Pat' model (a term coined by an adviser in the former Lothian region) is one where the decisions about who needs what are made at the centre – of the country, the local authority or the establishment – without any reference to the end-users and the package of activities is simply 'delivered'. The metaphor of 'delivery' emerged during the Technical and Vocational Education Initiative in the 1980s which identified certain skills and experiences which had to be delivered. Elements of this phenomenon had appeared in the early days of the Standard Grade development in the late 1970s, when groups were set up nationally to produce curriculum materials which would then be 'delivered' in classrooms across the country. However it was in CPD where it really reached its apotheosis.

Within what was the largest local authority in Scotland in the 1990s, the 'Postman Pat' model reigned supreme. Essentially, the Chief Advisers, working in collaboration with the Senior Advisers in the various divisions, would use the budgets allocated by the Scottish Office Education and Industry Department and targeted at specific curriculum areas, to mount a range of in-service courses. Within the divisions, there would be a similar process, and advisers would run courses for Principal Teachers or senior staff in primary schools. Only in a small number of cases would there be a mechanism for the recipients to participate in decisions about the agenda for such events. The in-service training was done to people rather than being done *with* them.

Thus the question is begged; whose needs are being met through CPD? Are the needs of the Local Authority – the employer – paramount? After all, they are funding the process and they are ultimately accountable for the quality of education. Should they reserve the right to determine the priorities for CPD? Is the ultimate aim of CPD to empower teachers to use their skills to promote effective learning? If so, should these same teachers have a part to play in the decisions which are made about the nature and quality of that CPD? As with many things in the field of education, the answer may well be – a bit of both. Indeed, a participatory approach to decision-making is at the other end of the continuum from the 'Postman Pat' model.

A strong centralist tradition

In 1992, the then Principal of Jordanhill College of Education (later to become the Faculty of Education of Strathclyde University), Dr Tom Bone, argued that:

compared with England, Scotland has always had a strong centralist tradition... In education, one example of it is the existence of a single examination board for Scotland, whereas England and Wales have been used for years to the situation of having many examination boards and the opportunity to choose among them... We set up a whole series of what I would call central agencies, like the Scottish Consultative Council on the Curriculum (SCCC) and its predecessor the Consultative Committee on the Curriculum (CCC); like the General Teaching Council (GTC); like the Scottish Council for Research in Education (SCRE); like, later, the Scottish Technical and Vocational Education Council (SCOTVEC); the Scottish Council for Educational Technology (SCET); and so on. Faced with something big and new that was happening, the natural way to deal with it in Scotland was to use a central agency.'

(Bone in Boyd, 1992: p. 30)

The role of the (S)CCC has been documented by Gatherer (1989) and, in particular, its early, emerging relationship with the Scottish Education Department:

There can be no doubt that the SED sees its (the CCC's) job as converting government policies into educational strategies, and converting its educational thinking into school programmes and materials.   (1989: p. 54)

The word 'materials' is important here since hitherto, there had been little in the way of centrally produced materials. Course books and primers had been the staple diet of pre- and post-war schools. Now, curriculum materials centrally produced and locally 'delivered' were to become a key element in the central strategy in a number of initiatives.

However, the SCCC was, as its name suggests, consultative in nature and could only make things happen with the agreement of the partner organisations, notably the local authorities. Andrew Chirnside, then Her Majesty's Depute Senior Chief Inspector, put it this way:

We would say, 'let's have a conference with the Directors of Education.' This could be on anything, school building, new primary schools, and other themes. So, there was an established relationship between the Department and the directorate to discuss items that had been agreed between them.

(Chirnside in Boyd 1992: p. 32)

This 'collusion' was all part of the way in which the 'policy community' (McPherson and Raab 1988) worked. Humes (1986) has characterised it as the workings of a 'leadership class', perpetuating its own value system, to the exclusion of others.

Although certainly centralist, it was by no means dictatorial. As Bone points out, there were checks and balances in the system:

> Government can never deliver by itself. It has to use other people. These people take the bits of the programme that comfortably fit into their background, experiences and assumptions. They take on a few of the others and they promote most strongly that which fits, and the teachers take on most strongly that which fits, and after a while the Government says, 'has this brought about what we wanted?
>
> (Bone in Boyd, 1992: p. 32)

However, events in the late 1970s and early 1980s were to change the political and educational landscape. The emergence of the New Right in the Thatcher Government and a period of industrial action among teachers in Scotland, would combine to make the centralist approach much more interventionist in character.

Standard Grade – five-year plans and great leaps forward?

1977 was an *annus mirabilis* in Scottish Education. Three major reports were published, two on the curriculum and assessment in S3 and S4 and one on truancy and indiscipline, in Scottish schools:

- *The Munn Report*   The Structure of the Curriculum in S3 and S4
- *The Dunning Report*   Certification and Assessment in S3 and S4
- *The Pack Report*   Truancy and Indiscipline

The groups had deliberated for some three years and in a co-ordinated move, produced their findings around the same time. Comprehensive education was by now well established throughout the country, and even those local authorities which had delayed its introduction for financial and logistical reasons, had by now made the move. The school leaving age had been raised in 1972 to 16; 'O Grades', introduced in 1962 for a minority of the pupil population, were now being extended to a much larger proportion of each S4 cohort; and the system was under severe strain.

The response by the Government was to set up three separate, but, theoretically, linked committees to examine aspects of the system. Scottish Education had not, since the 1947 Advisory Council, looked at the whole of the education system. Instead, it looked at bits of it. Sometimes it looked at the primary sector as a whole, as in *The Primary Memorandum* (1965). Sometimes it looked at aspects, such as vocational education, as with *The Brunton Report* (1963). But, in the 1970s, it began a process which was to last until the early twenty-first century, of looking at 'slices'. In 1974, even the slice of S3 and S4, narrow enough some might say, was further subdivided into Curriculum, and Assessment and Certification. The third of the national committees was to enquire into Truancy and Indiscipline, and although it may appear that its establishment in 1974 was merely coincidental, there was a realisation that among the reasons for truancy and indiscipline were an inappropriate curriculum and an examination system geared to an academic minority.

A full treatment of these major committees is not for this book, but, undoubtedly, of the three reports which emerged in 1977, those on Curriculum (*The Munn Report*) and Assessment and Certification (*The Dunning Report*) had the greatest impact on CPD. Essentially, the outcome of the two reports was the abolition of 'O' Grades and their replacement by 'Standard' Grades. These would be available to all S4 pupils at three levels:

- Credit
- General
- Foundation.

Thus, 'certification for all' became the slogan, and the comprehensive ideal of all pupils being educated together in one school, being able to gain formal and nationally validated recognition for their achievements, was to be realised. Theoretically, any pupil could sit up to seven (later eight) Standard Grades, at any combination of the three levels of Credit, General and Foundation. The advantages of the system were that no pupil would ever again be deemed 'non-certificate' and consigned to a sub-standard educational experience so eloquently denounced by pupils themselves in *Tell Them from Me* (Gow and McPherson 1980). Not only that, but the most able pupils, for whom the two-term dash to Higher in S5 was often simply too onerous, would now be able to reach a higher standard of achievement at Credit than hitherto possible even at A in 'O' Grade, thus enabling them to achieve more in S5. And, finally, the flexibility in the system (illustrated in Figure 8.1 from *The Dunning Report*) would enable pupils to be presented at the appropriate level across their subjects, from Foundation to Credit.

However, at school level, the debate was not so much about the levels or the philosophy underpinning the levels, it was about the courses which would need to be in place to meet the needs of pupils and to prepare them for the assessment, internal and external, which would determine which level of award they would eventually achieve.

For the first and only time in such a major national development, a Feasibility Study was mounted for Foundation level English and Maths. This was breaking new ground on a number of fronts. The concept of national certification for formerly 'non-certificate' pupils was itself novel. The idea that there should be a trialling of courses leading to the Foundation award was also ground-breaking. English and Maths departments in secondary schools up and down the country produced, shared and trialled new materials and new methods of teaching a course which would motivate and challenge pupils who had hitherto not had the chance to sit external examinations. There were national conferences led by HMCI Quentin Cramb which were the focus of a degree of creativity and altruism among Principal Teachers of English which was unprecedented.

By the end of the Feasibility Study in 1980, decisions had been taken to 'roll out' the Standard Grade programme to all subjects in all Scottish schools. A network of working groups was set up, chaired, in the main, by Advisers and supported by relevant subject specialists from HMI. Their main task was to produce materials and resources in a form which could be taken and implemented by classroom teachers across Scotland. These would, typically, be in the form of Units, fully 'fleshed out' and ready for use with S3 and, as the programme developed, S4. It had, indeed, become a 'Postman Pat' approach.

And it would probably have done the job, so to speak, had not the concerns among teachers about workload escalated into industrial action which included a ban on all new developments, including Standard Grade. 'Postman Pat', unwilling to cross the metaphorical picket line, was temporarily unable to make his deliveries. However, many of the groups continued to meet and when the dispute was settled the materials began to flood into the schools and into classrooms. In some cases, the quality of these materials was very high; in others, kit was more variable. The important thing from a CPD perspective was that Advisers in each Local Authority took a leadership role within their own subject specialism and provided in-service courses for secondary teachers for the implementation of Standard Grade. As a strategy for ensuring that a central curricular initiative was implemented in every school in the country, it was undoubtedly successful. As a way of empowering teachers and giving them ownership of the process of curriculum change, it was less impressive.

Ministerial fiats... and Rolls Royces

In their seminal work, *Governing Education*, McPherson and Raab (1988) quote the former Secretary of State for Scotland, Bruce Millan, as saying:

> I think, at the end of the day, the system does change, and change significantly, but it can't just be done by administrative or ministerial fiat, you know. It just doesn't work like that.
>
> (1988: p. ix)

He was not in any sense relinquishing Ministerial responsibility; he was simply acknowledging the reality that while Ministers may be able to set out a legislative framework, they cannot force teachers in classroom to comply. However, it could be argued that Michael Forsyth, a successor of Millan's Ministerial portfolio in the 1990s, had no such qualms. The period of protracted industrial action had left the Conservative Minister with a determination that never again would teachers thwart a Minister's policy agenda. The report, *Education 10–14 in Scotland*, was the first casualty (Boyd 2004). Its teacher-centred recommendations and its principle of 'professional autonomy within guidelines' were far too woolly-minded and liberal. He wanted action, not fine words (of which there were many in the

10–14 report) and he initiated a centrally driven policy initiative. 5–14 became the successor of 10–14 and it had an implicit threat of legislation behind it should the teaching profession fail to implement its standards-led strategy. Levels of pupil attainment A–E were centrally produced and Primary Testing (later National Testing) proposed to provide national benchmarks. Guidelines for every subject area were published after what many felt was cursory consultation. While the Guidelines did not have the force of statute (as the National Curriculum had in England and Wales), it soon became apparent that there were expectations that 5–14 would be implemented across the whole country in a similar manner.

The CPD which was to support 5–14 took on a special significance. Local Authorities were to be given Specific Grants to support such in-service training and the money was only payable provided the training met the priorities of the Guidelines. Room to manoeuvre was, therefore, limited, and most Local Authorities made central provision. Even when money was devolved to schools, the conditions circumscribing the devolution were such that training was often 'bought' from advisory staff and Colleges of Education, and the content was centrally driven. Indeed, the provision of such in-service training was akin to the centrally driven economies of the Iron Curtain in the 1950s and 1960s. Advisers and members of the directorate would devise the plans and submit them to the SOEID for approval. From time to time there would be pogroms, or rather, restructurings, of the bourgeoisie (the advisory service) and then there would be a great leap forward. In the largest authority, Strathclyde, there would often be an expectation that all of the schools would 'deliver' the curriculum in the same way, from Drumchapel to Dalmellington, from Rothsay to Rutherglen.

There was little room for individuality, improvisation or interpretation. Notwithstanding the non-statutory nature of the national Development Programme, the implementation proceeded lockstep, with the only hiccup being the issue of National Testing. Once the resistance to the original model of P4 and P7 testing was resolved (by extending tests to cover all of the 5–14 Levels but, importantly, leaving the decision about the timing of the testing of individual children to class teachers and schools), the development proceeded – and CPD was delivered to support the implementation.

But how would CPD reach the classroom? And once there, how would anyone know if it was making an impact? More cynically, would anyone care how well 5–14 was being implemented; was the emphasis simply to be on 'compliance'? The centralism implied by the 'Postman Pat' model meant that once the Guidelines documents had gone through the consultation phase and had turned dark blue around the edges, the push was on to make them happen. In Strathclyde an early strategy was to 'second' staff from schools to do an audit of the existing, commercial schemes used in schools for language and number. Then, a 'matching' exercise was carried out so that the schemes could be aligned with the 5–14 Strands, Programmes of Study and Levels. Next, any obvious gaps could be plugged and adjustments made to the schemes. This done, there would be regional conferences held to give senior staff an opportunity to explore the new guidance for schools, and then the six divisions which made up Strathclyde, for instance, would 'roll out' the new materials via CPD for staff in their schools.

This was a successful model if the key criterion was speedy implementation. Staff in schools, inundated with a seemingly endless flood of 5–14 documents, needed reassurance. They had been told, by HMI and by Ministers, that 5–14 was not 'new'. Rather it was just a consolidation of existing good practice and as such they did not need to throw out their existing curricula, but simply had to structure it in a more systematic way. The key imperative for Local Authorities became the provision of support to schools; particularly, in the early days, to primary schools, on whom the burden of implementation fell. To have said, 'let's consult widely on the rationale for each of the 5–14 curricular areas; let's engage in discussion about the range of new and innovative approaches which could be used to achieve the desired outcomes; and let's conduct some pilot projects which can then be evaluated and good practice shared' – would not have gone down well with a hard-pressed teaching profession.

Re-inventing the wheel and teacher choice

There has always existed a tension within the 'Postman Pat' model between patronising or even de-skilling teachers by giving them packages to deliver in their classrooms, and leaving them to 'work it out for themselves' and create their own teaching materials. The problems with the first of these alternatives have already been discussed above; the problems with the second include duplication of effort, re-invention of the wheel and, in extreme cases, a feeling among teachers that no one in the system is looking at the big picture. Politically, the second alternative has been problematic since the teachers' industrial action of the 1980s when 'development' work was boycotted and Standard Grade implementation was delayed. Indeed, it could be argued that it was this experience of teacher power which convinced Michael Forsyth that the 10–14 report should not be implemented because its principle of 'professional autonomy within guidelines' seemed too much like giving teachers control over the implementation process. The 5–14 system was his response, with its central direction of the curriculum (though still not statutory as in England and Wales), its Levels and its testing regime.

In Scotland, the main bulwark between teachers and the re-invention of the wheel scenario has been the Local Authority. Even after local government re-organisation in 1996 when thirteen regional councils became 32 unitary councils, with all the concerns about lack of economies of scale, the reality was that they continued to have a strategic role and quickly began to produce their own curricular initiatives and their own curricular material for use in their schools. The most common pattern was the formation of a working group, sometimes with membership which included outside bodies such as University Faculty of Education staff including researchers, but most commonly drawn from the establishments within the Authority. Materials would be designed, piloted and then produced. In most cases, the Authority would produce and distribute the resources, perhaps in ring-binder format, free to all its establishments, with a formal launch as part of a conference. Variations on the model would be where external bodies such as Learning and Teaching Scotland were involved as partners and the resultant distribution was national. In rarer cases, the materials would be bought in from existing initiatives from the UK or as far afield as North America, and training would be provided to council staff as part of the package.

In these ways, the local authority tried to protect its staff from having to re-invent the wheel, but tried to avoid the 'Postman Pat' model by involving (some of them) in the production of the materials, by involving them in piloting the materials and by offering CPD to support the initiative. Since 1996, a number of councils have taken the lead in certain areas of the curriculum and there has developed a system where councils will purchase from one another materials and in-service training, thus avoiding duplication at council level as well as at classroom level. The issue still remains problematic at national level. How does an organisation like Learning and Teaching Scotland try to ensure that good ideas are available nationally without itself being seen to impose a single approach on the profession? The answer is partly to work on projects with local authorities and others as partners and then to try to 'roll out' materials when they are ready to those who want to use them.

The failure of national roll-outs in the recent past has led to new determination to get it right. Two examples will suffice; the 'Assessment is for Learning' initiative and the 'Masterclass' approach to ICT. Both are nationally led but in partnership with local authorities. Key staff have been seconded to work under national guidance but at a local level. Funding has been identified to release key staff to take part in courses and conferences, and pilot projects have been set up around the country. Internationally renowned figures have been brought to Scotland to lead CPD events and money has been released to fund small-scale action research projects at school and classroom level. Neither initiative has yet reached the stage of mass coverage; instead the gradualist approach has been favoured, believing that in this way the chance of the new ideas becoming embedded are greater. No doubt, Michael Fullan would approve. In his model of the change process, the *initiation* phase is crucial and should not be rushed. The *implementation* phase will rarely be without its setbacks (the implementation dip) but they need to be overcome for the *consolidation* phase to be reached.

SUMMARY

The 'Postman Pat' model of in-service training meant that someone at the centre produced a package and the teacher was expected to 'deliver' it. Indeed, the Scottish tradition was a top-down and centralist model of change. The 1977 *Munn* and *Dunning Reports* saw a massive national strategy, supported by a new approach to CPD. The Feasibility Study was the first of its kind and the provision of materials to support new subject courses was efficient, if not always effective. The arrival of a

New Right Minister in the Scottish Office, after an acrimonious period of teacher industrial action, heralded a break with tradition in both curriculum development and the implementation process. Local Authorities, however, continued to develop their own versions of national initiatives and in recent years Learning and Teaching Scotland has had a key role to play. It would appear that the most recent national CPD strategies have sought to take account of the research evidence on the successful management of change.

POINTS FOR REFLECTION

1 Is there a dilemma in terms of whether the alternatives to the 'Postman Pat' model might actually result in teachers up and down the country simply re-inventing the wheel?

2 In a small country like Scotland, is the centralist model simply the most efficient way of ensuring that change takes place?

3 What do you think were the pluses and minuses of a 5–14 case-study in the implementation of change?

4 CPD – the 'cascade' model

> Send reinforcements, they're going to advance.
> Send three and fourpence, they're going
> to a dance.
> **(Anon)**

The Cascade model

The metaphor was quite a simple one. If there were a small number of people who had the knowledge, skills and expertise, they could simply train a slightly larger number who would in turn train others, and there would be a cascade effect. In a country as small as Scotland, it simply meant that national conferences or courses could be mounted for representatives from each of the Local Authorities. They would go back and run similar events for representatives of all of the schools affected by the curricular change or initiative. These representatives would then be expected to go back and train the members of their departments or school staff. What could be simpler or more cost-effective? The problem was, of course, that 'twixt the cup of the central expert and the lip of the classroom teacher, there was many a slip'. In other words, the message got diluted at every stage and the task of the 'trainer' became more challenging the closer the initiative got to the classroom. The original message became distorted, the level of enthusiasm decreased and the expertise in terms of 'training' was often over-estimated at school level.

There were other, more graphic, and slightly more cynical, metaphors around at this time. The 'mushroom effect' was often referred to in which teachers saw themselves being kept in the dark and having 'fertiliser' dumped on them. While this was an overstatement, it was partially true. The Cascade model was fatally flawed. It relied at each stage on the trainers to be skilled and knowledgeable enough to equip the next level of practitioners with the expertise to put the ideas encapsulated in the particular initiative into practice in the classroom. But, it failed to acknowledge that the gap between the policy-makers and the policy-implementers could be too wide. The former often made too many assumptions about what was possible in the classroom; the latter often failed either to see the point in the changes at all, or simply did not believe that it could be done.

The problem with the traditional models of CPD was that they often relied on people with little or no experience as in-service trainers to pass on the message about changes in the learning and teaching process. Logistics, and cost, prevented all teachers from getting the chance to attended national conferences or courses, first hand. These were often the preserve of senior promoted staff. Even today, when thinking about CPD is supposed to be more sophisticated, classroom teachers rarely if ever, get a chance to attend such sessions, except on a rather random and ad hoc basis. If one were to look at the number of days staff spend out of school at courses or conferences, it would be directly proportionate to the level of promoted post held by the individual. Ask any headteacher and he or she will complain about the number of days spent out of school on 'official' business, including CPD. Deputes, heads of department, and former Senior Teachers would be next in order, with classroom teachers at the bottom of the heap. (The one exception to this rule, paradoxically, is probationer teachers, as we shall see in Chapter 5.)

Thus, classroom teachers are always the recipients of the cascade effect. They are the mushrooms in the dark room and it is not difficult to see why CPD is not always regarded as an enlightening experience. Even when the CPD is in-house, the classroom teacher may have little say in decision-making about priorities. The present author spends around a third of his time leading school- and cluster-based CPD, normally during in-service days. It is not uncommon, for the decision to extend the invitation to come from the headteacher or the senior management team or, at best, a working group within the school with responsibility for CPD or Learning and Teaching or Raising Achievement. But, it remains very rare that the invitation has emerged after consultation with the whole staff. This almost certainly accounts for the less-than-enthusiastic welcome offered by some staff, a little cynical, perhaps, about CPD in general, wishing they were somewhere else, and underwhelmed by this so-called 'expert' from Strathclyde University who, in the words of the headteacher, 'needs no introduction'! Thus, even, when the model is face to face in a whole-school context, the lack of consultation causes problems.

It is worth considering how and when the Cascade model developed and, in so doing, explore why it is that lessons have only slowly been learned and why the system appears to have Cascade as its default position.

The Primary Memorandum: a case from the past

The 1965 *Primary Memorandum* is a good case-study from a number of perspectives. It was arguably the most momentous change in thinking about primary education in the twentieth century. As a result, it shaped the way many people to this day think about primary schools. Long after the 5–14 programme imposed a tight structure on the shape of the primary school curriculum, people outside of the system still refer to the 'integrated day' and think of the curriculum as a 'seamless robe'. Equally, concepts such as 'discovery learning' still persist in the minds of many people and 'topic work' as a strategy is still looked upon with some nostalgia in some quarters of the primary school sector. And yet, when HMI produced a report in 1981, some sixteen years after the publication of *The Primary Memorandum*, on practice across Scotland in P4 and P7, it appeared that the revolution had been more apparent than real.

An early commentator on the Scottish education system, Osborne, commented that the Scottish Education Department appeared to subscribe to the work of Piaget 'with all the appearance of having undergone a sudden conversion'. There was an inherent irony in a document which described the child as a learner in terms of 'natural curiosity and a desire to learn', but which itself sought to impose an ideology on the teaching profession. The Advisory Council, some twenty years earlier had warned, 'Pupils must not be conditioned to any set and predetermined way of thinking and acting.' (SED 1947: p. 5).

And yet here was a report which, apparently, sought to do just that. Nevertheless, with its insistence that the primary years were more than simply a preparation for secondary school, and with the recommended removal of the Qualifying Examination, the way was open for quite radical change in terms of the curriculum and methodology in the primary school.

A central issue raised by *The Primary Memorandum* was the locus of control in terms of decisions about what should be taught, when and in what ways. Gatherer (1989: p. 67) has argued that 'the teacher should decide, albeit under guidance'. The problem at this juncture was the gap in understanding of the implications of Piaget's theories for the classroom which existed between HMI and teachers. When HMI came to look at the impact of *The Primary Memorandum* on practice at P4 and P7, they concluded that:

> The message of this survey should be clear. Many of our teachers still feel threatened by the changes of recent years, yet they have maintained standards in those competences that are the key to progress on the part of their pupils. That this is not enough, however, is the message of this report.
>
> (SED 1981: p. 54)

Perhaps the most startling aspect of this conclusion is not the situation it describes but the fact that it is written, in the words of Edwin Morgan, from 'unironic lips'. The HMI take no responsibility for the apparent failure of the implementation of the report. Indeed their description of the status quo, circa 1980, reveals all:

> At the same time as our teachers appear to be better informed about their role and better supported by advice nationally and locally, they are more conscious of the gap between expectations and realisation, and are more prone to rely on tried and tested measures in those aspects in which Scottish primary education has been traditionally strong.
>
> (SED 1981: p. 54)

Farquharson (1990) has argued that policy-makers, working, perhaps, at a higher theoretical level, experience a 'paradigm shift' that is not matched by teachers who are closer in their thinking to 'the well informed citizen'. She suggests that 'the theoretical ideas of their pedagogy are rarely invoked in the work situation'. Indeed, she sees a fundamental tension when such theories as underpinned *The Primary Memorandum* are 'superimposed' on teachers' consciousness:

> child-centred education...is incompatible with a social structure characterised by capitalism and domination; it would impede the

> transmission of the cognitive style of passivity and dependency
> that ensures its maintenance and legitimisation.
>
> (1990: p. 36)

Farquharson saw the 5–14 programme with its imposition of National Testing as further evidence of a society unwilling to implement radical change in its system of schooling.

A less ideological analysis of the apparent failure of *The Primary Memorandum* to become fully implemented by 1981 is that the gap between the policy-makers and the policy-implementers was not, in fact, bridged by the appropriate levels and quality of CPD. Taken together these two analyses point to the fact that when teachers have imposed upon them change which they neither understand nor accept, there is little likelihood of any successful implementation without a model of CPD which enables them to make sense of the change and accommodate it within their existing framework of theory and practice.

Inclusion – a case from the present

The Primary Memorandum was published in 1965 and the HMI survey of progress in P4 and P7 came out in 1981. Standard Grade developments were underway, the 10–14 committee was about to be formed and 16+ Action Plan and TVEI were beginning to make an impact. Then, there was 5–14, Howie's report in 1994, *Higher Still – Opportunity for All* and New Community Schools, to name but a few. Surely the system, and those who managed it, would have learned lessons? The Cascade model doesn't work; does it?

In the late 1990s the establishment of a Scottish Parliament, coupled with local government reorganisation, saw a new emphasis on raising attainment and tackling social exclusion. Thus 'inclusion', became the buzz-word. Legislation incorporated it in 2000, building on the 1995 Children's Act and incorporating the United Nations Charter on the Rights of the Child. Terminology began to change also so that words like 'integration' were replaced by 'a presumption of mainstreaming' and, later, 'special educational needs' (SEN), in use since the *Warnock Report* of 1978, was replaced by 'additional support needs' in 2003. All of this would point to the fact that Inclusion was a sensitive and difficult issue, politically and emotionally charged, since the children being provided for were among the most vulnerable and the most challenging in the system.

If 'presumption of mainstreaming' were to result in more children being included in mainstream schools, and if 'raising attainment' were to be seen by those implementing the policy as complementary rather than inimical to inclusion, surely one predictable consequence would be that front-line staff (teachers, classroom assistants, other professionals working in and with schools) would require relevant and effective CPD?

Between 1999 and 2003, the present author, along with Paul Hamill of Strathclyde University, undertook three studies into aspects of Inclusion at local authority level. Two of these studies looked at inclusion of young people with Social, Emotional and Behavioural Difficulties (SEBD) and the other looked at provision for pupils with severe and complex learning needs. No matter the specific issue under review, the responses of the teachers to the questionnaire were fairly consistent. CPD, or the lack of it, was a major complaint.

Of the 54 items in the questionnaire, a small number attracted strong levels of agreement across teaching staff in all of the schools. In one authority where SEBD was the focus, in every school at least 20 per cent of the staff *strongly agreed* with the statement:

'Teachers feel the Inclusion initiative was imposed upon them.'

Indeed, in most schools the figure was around 50 per cent, rising to 65 per cent in two of them. As for areas of disagreement, all but one of the schools at least 20 per cent *strongly disagreed* in response to the statement:

'Adequate and appropriate continuing professional development
is provided for teachers in relation to Inclusion.'

In every case, the staff in the schools surveyed were given time (when Planned Activity Time was still available) to complete the questionnaire and were given the opportunity to write extended comments about the issue of Inclusion in general. They wrote of an absence of relevant CPD or a dearth of places on the small number of relevant courses available. Often, opportunities were given to specialist Support for Learning or Behaviour Support staff to take part in CPD or even to take award-bearing courses at University Faculties of Education. The problem was that these people were expected to go back to school and 'cascade' the training. This was often unrealistic. Not only does such an expectation underestimate the difficulty of leading colleagues and peers in training on such a controversial issue, but it ignores the level of expertise required to conduct in-service training with a professional audience.

The result of such a model of CPD, in the case of Inclusion, is a degree of cynicism among teachers which is difficult to ignore. At best, these teachers will harbour resentment about the position into which they have been put by policy-makers. At worst, they will grow cynical and lose sympathy for the pupils whose needs are the most challenging, irrespective of the fact that the policy on Inclusion has been forced on them too.

Training the trainers

If the Cascade model is generally regarded as ineffective, why does it keep reappearing, often in different guises? Part of the answer lies in the relationship between the centre and the periphery in Scottish education. As we have seen (Chapter One) the Scottish system has been described as 'centrally governed and locally administered', although some local government politicians have argued that this description underestimates the contribution of the Local Authorities in Scotland, which often initiates policy as well as implementing national policy. Nevertheless, national policies have been formulated for most major curricular issues and the major committees or working groups which have been formed to produce the policies have themselves often included key figures from Local Authorities. Once the policy has received the approval of the minister, the expectation is that it will be taken forward by a mix of national strategy and local support.

In the 1990s the strategy emerged of using Specific Grant funding from the Scottish Office Education and Industry Department (SOEID) given directly to Local Authorities. This money was, in the jargon, 'ring-fenced' and could only be spent on the initiative specified. Much of it was to fund CPD at regional level, with the lead being taken often by HMI who would mount national conferences at which all of the local authorities would be represented. A new variation on the Cascade model developed, namely, the 'training of trainers'. This would often involve the 'seconding' of leading Local Authority staff to work centrally, training others from Local Authorities, who would themselves often be seconded from their schools to work within their own local authority. In some cases, these people would work with key personnel from schools who would then take the message back to their colleagues. In others, these key staff would conduct whole-school or departmental in-service training as part of a rolling programme to disseminate the particular initiative to all schools.

Even at a time when resources were being delegated to schools as part of a drive to make Local Authorities enabling rather than controlling organisations, much of this Specific Grant funding was held centrally or, at the very least, 'top-sliced' to ensure that there would be a consistent approach taken across each local authority. In a real sense, the SOEID did not take much of an interest in how policies were implemented at Local Authority level, as long as they were implemented. Specific Grant funding was in one sense a control mechanism, a clear threat that if the money was not used for the specific purpose, it would be withdrawn. More insidiously, if the authority could not spend all of the money, it would receive a cut the following year. Thus, the money had to be spent!

Impact on the pupils' learning

What has never satisfactorily been quantified is the impact on pupils' learning of models which essentially mean that teachers have to leave the classroom to be 'trained'. Figures exist at Local Authority level of the number of teaching days lost through absence each year. These can be further subdivided into those lost through illness and those lost through attendance at CPD. Information exists at school level of the numbers of supply teachers employed to 'cover' such classes, and the numbers of times teachers in the school have had to do a 'please take' for a colleague who is out of school for CPD purposes. The problem is that no one collates these figures nationally. In an era where almost everything else is measured, statistics collected, collated and published, from pupil absence to free school meals entitlement to all kinds of test data, no one seems interested in measuring the extent of the disruption to pupils' learning of CPD.

Later, in Chapter 9, we will consider how the positive effects of CPD on pupils' learning can be evaluated, but at this stage the issue is the disruptive effects of models of CPD which rely on teachers leaving their pupils to attend courses and conferences in an off-site location. Since 1981, there have been five days set aside each year, called 'in-service days', when pupils are not in schools and whole staffs can engage in a range of CPD activities. Until 2002, these were supplemented by a number of Planned Activity Sessions (PAT); thereafter, as part of the McCrone Agreement, PAT was removed and replaced by an entitlement to 35 hours CPD per year for all staff, as we have seen in Chapter 1. But this was never envisaged as being the only CPD which would be offered. Each Local Authority offers its own menu of courses, some aimed at specific staff (for example, Principal Teachers, Senior Managers, CPD Co-ordinators, etc.) while others are on general offer; with people or schools opting in and sending interested members of staff.

Many of these staff are expected, as part of the school's CPD policy, to go back and lead in-service training with, or at least give feedback to, colleagues in school. While this may be more akin to Cascade than training of trainers, the basic model lives on. In South Lanarkshire Council every time there is a CPD course run under the auspices of the Council, whether the presenter is a member of its own staff or an external consultant, a form has to be completed in triplicate. As well as collecting information about the participants in terms of employment status (full/part time; permanent/temporary), age group, ethnic origin and disability, so that the Council can supply statistics to SEED, the form also allows the participants to make qualitative comments on the CPD activity. Issues around aims, needs, skills and knowledge, content and relevance are explored and ratings on a 1 to 4 scale are used. Most importantly of all is the section headed 'How will you apply today's learning to your job activities?' Here the participants are asked to consider:

- Changes to approaches to practice
- Further reading
- Share information with colleagues
- Improve/change systems or procedures
- Use new skills for a particular task
- Pass on learning to my team.

A copy of the completed form goes to the presenter, the line manager/CPD co-ordinator and to the participant's CPD Record.

It is the CPD co-ordinator who is the key person in this regard. He or she is the member of the senior management team charged with the responsibility of ensuring that each person who goes out of school for CPD adds value to the school as a result.

If 'cover' has had to be bought in to allow the member of staff to attend the course; if colleagues among the staff have had to give up valuable 'non-contact time' to cover their colleague's classes; if the person who goes out of school is not available to cover the classes of others – there has been a cost to the school (even if the course itself is 'zero-rated, i.e. free). Thus the school expects something in return in the sense that the participant will come back and share the fruits of the experience with others.

Cascade or trick(le)?

It could be argued that the cascade model has never really gone away; it has simply become more bureaucratic. Now, every CPD activity has to be evaluated, recorded and future intentions articulated. The expectation is that CPD must make an impact not only on the practice of the individual but on the establishment in which s/he works. Quite how this is done will be examined later, but the question arises as to how the person can be given time and support in order to share the practice. The real danger is that the individual simply gets swamped on return to the classroom, and the next opportunity to share the original experience may be too far away to be relevant. One individual may be able to make a difference on immediate colleagues, in a stage or in a department, but it is difficult to see how, without careful planning and a well constructed whole-school policy, an impact can be made on the whole establishment.

The question of measurement arises also. How will we know if there has been an impact on, for example, pupil learning? Will it be measured in terms of examination or test results? Could it be less quantitative and be more to do with pupil engagement and motivation? What would the criteria be and who would do the measuring? In other words, the theory of cascade seems quite simple but the ability to determine if it actually makes a difference to the practice of the participant or the pupils of the participant, is less apparent. Perhaps the trickle effect is more accurate a description. As each member of staff comes back from CPD activities, perhaps enthused, inspired or invigorated, then the school may be able to identify a 'critical mass' of such staff who, perhaps as part of a working group or planning committee, can shape in-school CPD activities.

Indeed, the trickle effect may, in the longer term, have a greater possibility of success. It may be closer to the reality of the change process itself. As Fullan (1992) has suggested, the Initiation phase of the change process is one which should never be rushed. The longer change takes to be discussed, piloted and evaluated, the more likely the subsequent stages of Implementation and Consolidation will be successful. Thus, no one person should carry the burden of expectation as change agent, but should be supported by others, especially senior staff, to ensure that change becomes embedded in the everyday practice of staff in the school.

Now the deluge?

The economics of CPD will always mean that when courses or conferences come along and schools want to send staff to them to support aspects of the school development plan, it is highly unlikely that more than one or two staff will be able to be released at the same time. The costs to the school include not simply the conference or course fee, but also the cost of bringing in staff to cover the classes of the absent teachers. There are also opportunity costs. Will the cover or supply teachers be of a high quality, experienced and motivated enough to ensure that the work of the classes is not disrupted. If the staff going on the CPD activity are senior staff, there may be fewer classes to cover, but if situations arise during the day which require the intervention of senior staff, it can be just as disruptive to the life of the school.

Some schools have tried to shift the balance of CPD activities from centrally provided courses to in-school activities, not exclusively but at least to the extent of trying to reduce disruption of classes. The positive aspect of such a shift is to capitalise on the expertise of staff themselves. Thus schools like St Aidan's High School North Lanarkshire or Trinity High School in Carlisle, have begun to use their own staff to lead in-service training. This may take the form of teaching model lessons in front of colleagues during an in-service day (Trinity) or departmental heads making presentations to colleagues about aspects of good practice (St Aidan's). In many primary schools and pre-5 establishments, the idea of teachers and, increasingly, classroom assistants leading in-service training for colleagues, is well established. Indeed, in some schools, albeit the minority, staff from the whole cluster will come together for an in-service day on an aspect of learning and teaching, and good practice will be shared.

The idea is that teachers can learn from one another, can share their expertise and create a 'critical mass' of staff who are willing to try new approaches. The theory is that such an approach to change, while still having elements of the cascade model, means that no one individual will be expected to carry the whole burden of disseminating the message of a course or conference. Instead, groups of teachers working within or across departments or stages, are pooling their expertise, embedding the changes within their day-to-day practice and, most importantly, being in a position to evaluate the impact of the new approaches. It is less likely, therefore, that lessons from CPD will be seen as quick fixes or fads, and more likely that they will be consolidated within the practice of the school.

Thus, the overall balance of CPD changes. In-service days become an integral part of the dissemination process and the expertise of teachers within the school is used to ensure that the new ideas build on work already going on in classrooms.

Psychologically, it suggests that it is the staff within the school who become the 'experts' rather than 'gurus' from Universities who, instead, complement the work of the school. Given that teachers have the hard-edged experience of teaching and academics have access to the latest research and theory, their relationship becomes symbiotic. Rather than going out of school to be told how to teach more effectively, teachers can engage with new ideas, bring them back to their colleagues, locate the good practice which undoubtedly will already exist within the school and then set about using the in-service time which the school has at its disposal to spread the practice across the school. The cascade model has been transformed and the school has taken ownership of the process of change.

SUMMARY

The cascade model, from the point of view of the policy-makers seemed efficient and cost-effective. Training a few who would go on to train the many, however, did not prove to be acceptable either to the trainers or to the trained. Examples from the past and present show the problems associated with the model. *The Primary Memorandum*, some fifteen years after publication was not being implemented satisfactorily according to HMI because of a policy-making/implementation gap. In modern times recent research suggests that Inclusion is being hampered because teachers do not feel that they have been adequately trained to meet pupils' additional support needs. A key question remains as to whether pupils' learning is improved by their teachers' CPD. Schools and Local Authorities now try to assess the impact on practice of teachers' involvement in CPD. While the Cascade model has not entirely disappeared, the next challenge is the 'deluge' which will come with the requirement for all teachers to do 35 hours CPD. How will the system ensure that all of this activity will contribute to more effective learning and teaching in schools?

POINTS FOR REFLECTION

1. Do you have any experience of the Cascade model? What advantages and disadvantages have you found with it?

2. *The Primary Memorandum* and Inclusion have been offered as examples. Do you think they illustrate any particular aspects of the Cascade model. Do you have any other examples from your own experience?

3. How does the organisation you work for try to assess the impact of CPD on student learning?

4. Is there, post McCrone, a danger of there being too much CPD? Could it amount to overload or do the advantages outweigh the disadvantages?

5 CPD – and the reflective professional

> In the middle of a particularly busy day, the emperor was driven to a meeting hall for an appointment of some kind. But when he arrived, there was no one there. The emperor walked into the middle of the great hall, stood silently for a moment, then bowed to the empty space. He turned to his assistants, a large smile on his face. 'We must schedule more appointments like this,' he told them. 'I haven't enjoyed myself so much in a long time.
>
> *The Tao of Pooh*, B. Hoff

Time to think

Everybody needs time to think, even emperors! David Schon (1983) coined the term 'reflective practitioners', namely teachers who value the opportunity to explore their practical professionalism in different, structured situations. David Hartley, however has questioned the use of the word 'practitioner', arguing that it demeans the professionalism of teachers, casting them in the role of technicians. Perhaps the most accurate term, for the moment, therefore, is 'reflective professional'? Yet another David, Kolb, has extended Schon's ideas a little and described a process which he calls 'experiential learning' and his cycle promoted the notion of reflection on everyday practice:

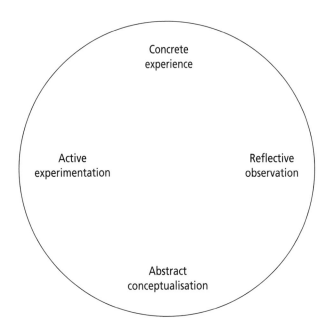

However we conceptualise the process of reflection, each of these three educational thinkers would agree that teachers ought to be reflective if they are to fulfil their potential as teachers and if they are to be fulfilled in their careers.

The role of CPD in helping teachers to become more reflective is seen as pivotal by many writers on the subject. Indeed, the attention which has been given to teachers-as-learners has built on a line of thinking which has been developing for the last 30 years. Adult learning has spawned its own body of theory, and just as *pedagogy* is the body of theory which relates to the teaching of children and young people, *androgogy* is the equivalent when applied to adult learning. Whitaker (1993) suggests that when we consider CPD we should take account of the following ten principles for adult learning:

- Voluntary participation
- Mutual respect
- Collaboration
- Action and reflection
- Organisational setting
- Choice and change
- Social, economic and cultural factors

- Motivation
- Critical thinking
- Self-direction.

Whitaker goes on to expand on how each of these principles has implications for the ways in which adult learning should be promoted in an educational CPD context. The only adaptation necessary to his model in the current Scottish context is that CPD is no longer voluntary; it is an entitlement – 35 hours have to be undertaken by every teacher in addition to the five in-service days which every school has each year and in addition to any courses which are attended within the school day.

1 Teachers are voluntary participants in professional development; they engage in it as a result of personal choice.

2 A relationship of mutual respect needs to be established between participants and tutors if the optimum conditions for effective learning are to be established. It is also essential for tutors to recognise that they too are learners, capable of learning from the different experiences of course members.

3 Adult learning is a collaborative experience and needs to be viewed by tutors as a relationship of equals.

4 A vital feature of adult learning is the process of action and reflection – looking back on past experience in order to make decisions about the future.

5 INSET tutors need to remember that most professional activity in education takes place in an organisational setting. This adds complexities and special challenges to the process of change.

6 In adults, personal and professional change can be difficult and painful. As a result of previous experience, some adults find it very hard to accept help and guidance. Trying to change their ways of working can involve loss of confidence and self-esteem.

7 Differences in the social, economic and cultural backgrounds of course attenders need to be respected and taken account of in designing and developing INSET activities.

8 The motivation to learn is a key consideration. Professional adults bring a wide variety of needs, hopes and aspirations to their own professional development.

9 One of the most valuable contributions a tutor can make to this learning partnership is to promote and facilitate a climate of critical thinking in which course members are encouraged to lay open to examination their professional thinking and practice.

10 A key aim of those involved in adult learning is to encourage self-direction. This involves gradually reducing dependence on the tutor and supporting the learner's own aspirations, learning strategies and self-evaluation.

(1993: p. 53–4)

If we accept these principles outlined by Whitaker, it is easy to see why simplistic models such as 'Postman Pat' and Cascade are flawed. The business of conducting CPD with professional teachers is such that it requires not merely a set of skills different from those needed to teach pupils successfully, but it presupposes a set of attitudes and ways of working which not everyone has. Ask any teacher who has led in-service training with colleagues in a school setting and he or she will tell you how daunting a prospect it is. An audience of one's peers is by far the most difficult to engage with and it is the principle that such an activity takes place in a community of equals which makes it so. The relationship among the tutor and the participants is a complex one, especially if they work together on a daily basis. The last thing a teacher wants to do is to give the impression to colleagues that s/he has all the answers, or is an 'expert' or somehow knows better than others.

However, Michael Fullan (1999), in his writings on educational change, proposes a collaborative model which suggests that the balance of CPD needs to shift towards in-school provision. He advances five characteristics of 'collaborative cultures for complex times':

> **Collaborative culture:**
> Fosters diversity while trust-building
> Provokes anxiety and contains it
> Engages in knowledge creation (tacit to explicit, explicit to tacit)
> Combines connectedness with open-endedness
> Fuses the spiritual, political and intellectual.
> (*Fullan, Change Forces: the Sequel*, 1999: p. 37)

Fullan and Stiegelbauer (1991: p. 117) go further and put teachers at the heart of the improvement process: 'Educational change depends on what teachers do and think – it's as simple and as complex as that.' If teacher thinking is important, how does a collaborative culture promote reflection?

Reflection – with a little help from my friend?

Brown (1989) re-inforced the idea of teacher as reflective professional, but, in doing so, underlined how difficult it is for even the most experienced – and most skilled – teachers to reflect on their own teaching, even immediately after the event. In the white-hot heat of the classroom, how much of what teachers do is intuitive, derived from years of experience, with minute-to-minute decisions sometimes occurring at a sub-conscious level. Even when planning has been detailed and organisation excellent, subtle shifts in relationships, emphasis and attitudes take place in every lesson.

My own experience as a teacher would support this view. As a young Principal Teacher of English, I had a student from Jordanhill College of Education observing my S2 class. The class was mixed ability and had three boys in it whose behaviour could be challenging. They 'needed watching'. The lesson was part of a sequence on the theme of Animals and after an introduction, I embarked, in response to a question, on a detailed description of a bullfight (the one and only bullfight) I had watched in Spain. Thereafter, the pupils embarked on activities which formed part of the Unit on Animals.

At the end of the lesson, the student informed me that he had been using a detailed observation schedule to record the progress of the lesson. Mildly surprised, I asked him what he had observed. He informed me that during the first ten minutes or so of the introduction to the lesson, I had interrupted myself eleven times to say something to one or all of these three boys. I had either simply mentioned one of them by name to ensure attention or had make a specific remark ('pay attention', 'face the front' or 'can I have your full attention?'). However, he said, during the next fifteen minutes in which I gave a graphic account of the bullfight, there had been not one interruption! As I digested this information, he asked, 'So, what do you conclude from that?' I said, ironically, 'that I was boring for the first ten minutes?' 'My thoughts entirely,' he concurred.

I should say that we went on to become good friends and colleagues and that he is now a Depute Headteacher, but I was, I have to admit, taken aback. I simply would have had no idea of my own behaviour without the benefit of his astute observation!

The idea that teachers should engage in collaborative activity which would be part of a broader definition of CPD is not new.

Fullan has adapted a range of analyses of continuing professional development into the following tripartite model:

Assessment of Learning	Professional Learning Community	Pedagogical Practice

He has suggested that we view them as overlapping circles, with Assessment of Learning and Pedagogical Practice each contributing to the goal of the Professional Learning Community. In essence, Fullan argues, the internal workings of successful schools are key because in those which are truly learning communities, teachers:

- Pursue a clear purpose for all student learning.
- Engage in collaborative activity to achieve their purpose.
- Take collaborative responsibility for pupil learning.

(p. 72)

The challenge for schools arising from Fullan's ideas is not insignificant. There are structural issues to be overcome if schools are to adopt his collaborative model, particularly with respect to CPD. In some establishments, especially pre-5 and primaries, collaborative cultures already exist. Staff share good practice, observe one another's teaching, lead CPD activities for colleagues in areas where they have expertise and, generally, take a whole-school approach to all aspects of learning and teaching. Secondary schools find this more difficult to achieve because of the departmental structure and the more hierarchical nature of the organisation. But even here, some schools have gone a long way towards the kind of sharing Fullan would propose. It can be a slow process, involving imaginative timetabling arrangements to enable staff to 'shadow' a class for a day or observe (and be observed by) a colleague for a morning. It also involves a collaborative approach to the planning and delivery of in-service days, with staff being involved in identifying the issues as well as leading the sessions or even teaching 'sample' lessons for colleagues. These are all difficult things to manage and can be expensive, if, for example, classroom observation or shadowing necessitates the buying-in of a cover teacher.

The payback is, however, likely to be considerable. Newmann and Wehlage (1995) found that a school-wide professional community affected the level of:

- Classroom authentic pedagogy, which in turn affected student performance.
- Social support for student learning, which in turn affected student performance.

(p. 46)

Fullan contrasts these collaborative cultures with what he calls 'balkanised' schools where departments or stage teams work in isolation from, or even in competition with, others in the school. Often they are at loggerheads with one another, refuse to share common problems or pursue common solutions, and cynicism is often the prevailing attitude to the suggestion of change. Management and leadership can inhibit or enable collaboration, and a culture where department is played off against department or where 'heroes' and 'villains' are identified, is unlikely to promote collaboration.

Leadership, development planning and school culture

If time to think is a key element of successful CPD, then one of the goals of leadership must be to create opportunities from within the constraints of time, budgets and competing claims. And if leadership is not the preserve of the few within any healthy organisation but should be widely distributed among the staff, then leadership and CPD become inextricably linked. CPD must be an integral part of the development of leadership qualities and skills, while leaders must see CPD as part of their armoury in motivating others.

O'Brien, Murphy and Draper (2003) have suggested that leadership is a key issue for all staff and are moved to record their 'surprise that the Chartered Teacher development in Scotland...makes no direct provision for development in leadership.' They point the finger of blame at the teacher unions who, they claim, are 'so suspicious of the possibility that Chartered Teachers might be used to undertake management tasks in schools' that they have blocked any Modules which have a leadership element to them. Considering that the authors of the book are all, to some extent, involved in the promotion of leadership as a subject of postgraduate study and are, indeed, providers of such programmes, it may be that they are no more neutral in their observations than the unions they berate.

O'Brien *et al.* go on to quote the official agreement on teachers' conditions of service, Annex D:

> All teachers will have the right to be fully involved in the development of the school plan and to be consulted on their contribution to the plan, and the responsibility for realising the school's development Priorities.
>
> (2003: p. 55)

Given that CPD is an integral part of any such planning process, this might be one area where O'Brien and the teaching unions would agree. If taking the lead in developing aspects of the school plan, in delivering some of the CPD activities within it, in sharing good practice across subjects and stages and in collaborating in the improvement of learning and teaching, all add up to leadership, then this is indeed common ground. The difference exists only in the means to that end. O'Brien and his colleagues want leadership to be developed through postgraduate programmes, as in the Chartered Teacher programme, while Fullan might suggest that it is in how schools operate as organisations which will have the greatest impact. Ideally, it would be a mix of both.

In *The Empowered School* (1993), Hargreaves and Hopkins extol the virtues of school development planning as a collaborative process. They argue that development planning is a 'process of *learning*' [original emphasis]. They cite three main gains from this learning:

- Outcomes of planning.
- The enhancement of expertise.
- The revitalisation of the school's culture.

  (1993: p. 79)

Hargreaves and Hopkins argue that 'better staff development, which links individual professional development with institutional improvement' is one of the outcomes of the planning process, while the enhancement of expertise manifests itself in an increased capacity to 'deploy the talents and dedication of all involved through collaboration'. It is the culture of the school which is transformed most dramatically by a collaborative approach to development planning in their view by:

- Promoting a shared vision for the school.
- Creating management arrangements that empower.
- Providing for every teacher a role in the management of the school and opportunities for leadership.

- Encouraging everyone involved to have a stake in the school's continuing improvement.
- Generating the commitment and confidence which springs from success.

(1993: p. 79)

CPD, in many ways, is the linchpin of school improvement according to most recent research. It is at the heart of development planning, of a collaborative culture and is the means whereby staff at all levels can develop leadership skills. Ironically, it is only very recently in Scotland that CPD has been recognised formally by the system. Given that practice at a local school level takes time to catch up with the ideal which is promoted by educational thinkers, it is safe to say that a lot of work still remains to be done to put CPD at the heart of the matter. It may have become an entitlement for all teachers, but it has not yet been embraced enthusiastically all members of the profession.

Becoming a better teacher

Ultimately, the point of all CPD is to help teachers to become better at what they do. This begs two important questions: 'What makes a good teacher?' and 'How do you become a better teacher?' These are not easy questions to answer. For many years, when I did in-service training with teachers someone would inevitably ask the question, 'Are good teachers born, or are they made?' It was, almost invariably, posed as a challenge, and I always felt that my answers were unconvincing. However, more recently, having given the matter more thought, I have arrived at an answer which I thinks comes closer to the truth – 'They have to be born first!' In other words, no one is born a teacher. We all have to learn to become a teacher and that learning never stops throughout our careers. We never reach that day when we wake up and say, 'I'm now the perfect teacher. I can teach any and every class successfully.' Some people might have skills, attributes or even personality traits which predispose them to be more naturally good teachers, but they may not, in the longer term, be the most effective teachers. The outgoing, gregarious extrovert may not be as effective as the quiet, reserved, low-key introvert.

Part of the difficulty lies in the multi-faceted role of the teacher. Teacher as 'blackboard artist, show-off, comedian, ring-master, clown' was one 1970s definition, but this has to be placed alongside teacher as 'patient, sensitive helper of individuals.' In truth, we want our best teachers to be both, when the situation demands it.

There are many sources of advice on the characteristics of a good teacher. In Scotland in recent years we have had the development of 'competences' at various levels. Firstly, there is a set of competences for the emerging teacher. All those who seek to become teachers, primary or secondary, via the B.Ed. degree or the one-year postgraduate course, have to meet the standard as set out *Quality Assurance in Initial Teacher Education* (2000) This consists of a set of Standards, each one of which has a number of Benchmarks and Expected Features

When student teachers are assessed by tutors or by staff within the school where they are placed, it is against this standard that they are judged. Christie (2003: p. 936) has argued that 'course planners have in general been comfortable with these guidelines since the definition given of competence is not a narrow one.'

There are other competences which relate to the school situation. The current standard which applies to 'full registration' (*Achieving the Standard for Full Registration*, 2003) ought to articulate with the initial teacher education competences. Indeed, there is a section within the document which lays out 'How the SFR Links to the Standard for ITE'.

The *Standard for Chartered Teacher* (2002) has a different, more discursive format, which expands on each of four 'central professional values and commitments':

- Effectiveness in promoting learning in the classroom.
- Critical self-evaluation and development.
- Collaboration and influence.
- Educational and social value.

(SED 2002: p. 1)

Management competences, derived at least in part from the world of business and commerce, were the precursor of the Scottish Qualification for Headship. The *Standard for Headship in Scotland* (2000) sets out a Key Purpose for Headship, a set of three Professional Values (around Values, Learning and Knowledge), four Management Functions (Managing Learning and Teaching, Managing People, Managing Policy and Planning and Managing Resources and Finance) and, finally, a set of Professional Abilities, Interpersonal and Intellectual.

Theoretically, there should be progression throughout the professional life of teachers. The value of such an approach is often stated in terms of consistency and coherence. The competences are the fruits of the deliberations of some of the most experienced educationists in Scotland and have been the subject of consultation. They represent, in theory at least, the accumulated wisdom of the educational community.

However, there have been dissenters. Some commentators have been sceptical of the competence-based approach. They argue that it is instrumental, mechanistic and utilitarian. It does not reflect the complexity of the teaching process and does not sufficiently recognise the importance of values and philosophy. Not only that, it limits the possibilities, reduces the scope for inventiveness and militates against risk-taking. Far from being an enabling framework, the competences become, at worst, a straitjacket, trying to define and confine the roles which teachers play. Perhaps the problem lies less with any individual Standard than the inflexibility of any such list of characteristics. What is needed is a dynamic tool, one which the teacher can use, in collaboration with colleagues, to help her/him move towards a greater level of professional confidence. However, it is also inescapable that Standards also fulfil a benchmarking function, and can be used when issues of *in*competence arise. The question is whether the same Standard can fulfil both functions.

Perspectives on teacher competence – listening to pupils?

Research into pupils' perspectives on teachers and on schools has a proud history in Scotland and in the UK as a whole. Gow and McPherson published the ground breaking *Tell Them from Me* in 1980. Derived from the School Leavers' Survey, it told a divided story of pupils' experience of schooling. The last survey of its kind before the abolition of 'O' Grades, it demonstrated that non-academic, non-certificate pupils in Scottish secondary schools felt that they had had a raw deal, getting the worst teachers, being the first to be sent home if there was a teacher shortage and being 'sacrificed' in favour of the more prestigious, academic pupils. The book was explosive and caused shock waves throughout the system.

In England and Wales, Rudduck and others were exploring the pupil perspective on schooling. She argued that:

> We would go so far as to argue that there is an educational pay-off for young people, as well as for their schools, in providing opportunities for dialogue about learning – not just dialogue about personal problems and patterns of progress but also about school structures and issues in teaching and learning.
>
> (1996: p. 9)

More recently, a number of Scottish studies (Hamill and Boyd, 2000; Boyd and Lawson, 2003) have demonstrated that pupils' views on education are worth listening to. In particular, they have insightful things to say about the characteristics of an effective teacher. In *Schools Speak for Themselves* (MacBeath *et al.* 1986), the views of primary, secondary and special school pupils on what makes a good teacher were collated into what became known as the 'Mother Theresa Charter'; no teacher could aspire to have all of these characteristics all of the time.

The good teacher:

- is kind
- is generous
- listens to you
- encourages you
- has faith in you
- has time for you
- keeps confidences
- likes teaching children
- likes teaching their subject
- takes time to explain things
- helps you when you're stuck
- tells you how you're doing
- allows you to have your say
- makes sure you understand
- helps people who are slow
- doesn't give up on you
- cares for your opinion
- makes you feel clever
- treats people equally
- stands up for you

- makes allowances
- tells the truth
- is forgiving.

(1986: p. 54)

These views of pupils were reiterated in the study of pupils' views on Guidance commissioned by Inverclyde Council (Boyd and Lawson). Here pupils in secondary pupils were asked what makes a good Guidance teacher. Their views were remarkably consistent across the four schools.

Someone:

- who talks to you
- to whom you can talk freely
- who listens*
- who is about the place
- who is happy not grumpy
- who knows what is going on
- who trusts you
- who keeps confidences
- who does not interfere unnecessarily
- who has a sense of humour
- who is nice
- who is helpful*
- who is there when you need them
- who is smart
- who is confident
- who is normal
- who is approachable*
- who is friendly*
- who is male/female – as appropriate
- who is trustworthy
- who is non-judgmental
- who does not put you under pressure
- who can offer good advice
- who understands people of our age
- who talks to you like a person
- who doesn't shout at you
- who lays it on the line when necessary
- who helps you to understand
- who follows through.

(Boyd and Lawson 2003: pp. 177–8)

When asked what characteristics some teachers lacked which would debar them from being Guidance staff, their views were no less consistent:

- Lack of patience
- Uncaring
- Unfriendly
- Shouts
- Aggressive
- Hygiene
- Unable to relate to pupils
- Not approachable
- Unqualified
- Uncaring
- Poor communicator
- Sarcastic
- Unwilling to weigh up evidence
- Unwilling to take on extra responsibility.

(Boyd and Lawson 2003: p. 178)

The question is can these views which pupils have to offer be fed into teachers' CPD? Confident teachers would have no real problem in doing so, not least because the overwhelming majority of school pupils in Scotland, even a substantial proportion of the 'disaffected', like school and are positive about their experiences. The Ethos Indicators produced by HMI in the early 1990s, were predicated on the assumption that teachers', parents' and pupils' views of what a school was trying to do were all-important and that schools should be aware of the perceptions of all of its 'stakeholders'. In Chapter 9 we will look at some examples of how schools are developing their approach to CPD, and how some of them are building into that process regular surveys of the views of their key stakeholders. The rise of 'citizenship' as an issue for schools suggests that pupils should be more involved in decision-making and the concept of the 'democratic school' and the 'democratic classroom' are regarded by their proponents as an important way of producing citizens for the twenty-first century who actively promote democracy.

SUMMARY

Most writers on the subject of the reflective teacher put CPD at the heart of what they do. Indeed, just as there is *pedagogy* relating to learning and teaching of pupils and students, *androgogy* sets out the principles which should underpin adult learning and should, therefore, inform CPD. Many writers, most notably Michael Fullan, have argued that CPD should be a collaborative process and should contribute to a collaborative culture throughout the school. In recent years, there has been an increasing focus on leadership in education, either at headteacher level or more widely distributed across the school. One common factor is the promotion of a shared vision within the establishment. A key focus of CPD is to help teachers to become better at what they do. To this end, standards or sets of competences have been devised from Initial Teacher Education through Full Registration, Chartered Teacher and on to Headteacher in an attempt, not without controversy, to define the skills, qualities, values and dispositions of teachers at different stages in their careers. As a counterbalance to these official pronouncements on the qualities of teachers, there is growing evidence that listening to pupils' voices is important if school improvement is the aim of CPD.

POINTS FOR REFLECTION

1 What is your understanding of the term 'reflective professional'?

2 How would Whitaker's principles of adult learning fit with conventional approaches to CPD, in your experience?

3 What do you see as the potential benefits and problems associated with a more collaborative approach to CPD?

4 In what ways can experienced teachers become better at what they do?

6 CPD in the post-McCrone era: A question of quality?

> Those who can, do; those who can't, teach; those who can't teach, teach teachers.
>
> **(Old teacher proverb, based on G. B. Shaw quotation)**

Teaching in the twenty-first century – a new era for CPD?

We have already seen how CPD has become an entitlement for all teachers and traditional definitions have changed. The range of activities acknowledged as CPD had widened and there is the beginning of a shift from externally provided, centrally based CPD towards a more balanced approach where in-house, teacher-led CPD is given equal status to other forms. There is also now the notion of career-long CPD, beginning with pre-service training, through the probationary year, then either Chartered Teacher or other forms of CPD, formal and informal, until some of the profession embark on the Scottish Qualification for Headship. The view of the McCrone Committee, articulated in their report *A Teaching Profession for the 21st Century*, was that CPD was at the heart of teacher professionalism. The question for us now is whether the vision can be turned into reality.

The probationary year

In Scotland the probationary period was traditionally two years in duration. Up until the 1990s, this typically meant that the newly qualified teacher would spend it in one school. The General Teaching Council was charged with ensuring the quality of the experience and the validation of the professional competence of the teacher. The school would act as the agent insomuch as it would ensure that the teacher gained experience of the range of classes and the subject(s) in which he or she was qualified to teach. The head of department in the secondary, or the relevant member of promoted staff in the primary school would oversee the progress of the teacher and would, on a number of occasions, observe the teacher teaching. A pro forma would be completed, signed by the relevant people, including the teacher, and sent off to the GTC. In due course, the teacher would receive confirmation of the granting of full registration. In cases where there was doubt about the suitability of the teacher, there might be an extension of the probationary period; in more extreme cases, registration might not be granted. Thus, in theory, it was a partnership between school and GTC, and ultimately between the Local Authority, as employer, and the GTC.

There was very little explicit reference in this process to CPD. As a young teacher qualifying from the 1970s onwards, access to CPD was patchy, at best. With any luck, the teacher might get to go on a course, within, or more probably, outwith the school day. An ambitious young teacher might enrol, at her own expense, on an M.Ed. course run in the evenings at a university. Or, there might be an invitation to join a working party. These were all good opportunities for CPD, but essentially they were random and not open to everyone. Since McCrone, there has been a national commitment to a reduction of the probationary period to one year and a *guarantee* of CPD. Probationary teachers used to get a full teaching timetable in most schools; now, they must teach no more than 0.7 (70%) of the week. And, a significant proportion of that, typically, 0.2 (20%) of the week, is given to CPD. Thus in a year, probationer teachers might get the equivalent of six weeks of CPD. Only a couple of decades before, this is more than a probationary teacher might have done in ten years.

The implications of this development may be significant and long lasting. Expectations of new teachers may well be such that the quality of staff development will inevitably be raised. 'How're we gonna keep them down on the farm, after they've seen Paris?' could become the theme tune of Local Authorities as they try to build on the probationary year and create a coherent system of CPD. It will be a responsibility of school managers also to ensure that these new teachers' CPD needs are met through a well thought-out programme of school-based in-service training, building on the offerings of the Local Authority. Their expectations will be different from those of their colleagues who joined the profession a decade or more earlier. The lid has been lifted from the Pandora's Box, and things may never be the same again.

The new generation of probationer teachers now have new pathways to follow. They may decide to pursue a career by moving upwards through the promoted post structure, through Principal Teacher, to Depute Headteacher and, ultimately, Headteacher. For this they will need, in addition to their CPD portfolio, to engage in CPD courses which lead to postgraduate qualifications. This will be formalised as they approach the senior management stratum and the Scottish Qualification for Headship (SQA) is required. Should they decide to stay in the classroom and eschew the management route, the only option in terms of career advancement is Chartered Teacher which also requires postgraduate-level study, but with a clear focus on classroom practice. Either way, CPD is an essential component. We will now look in detail at the likely implications for CPD of these two initiatives.

Chartered Teacher – origins and early signs

The Chartered Teacher concept was born in the *McCrone Report* but had a long gestation period. For many years, the consensus in Scottish Education was that there needed to be a route for teachers to pursue their career without going down the management route. The idea that by staying in the classroom, taking additional postgraduate qualification and demonstrating expertise in teaching one could earn a salary equivalent to that of a head of department, had at last found its time. But how would it work in practice?

In *The Chartered Teacher* (Kirk *et al.* 2003) the authors trace the development of the chartered teacher back to the *Sutherland Report on Teacher Education and Training* of 1997, which recognised that in Scotland, CPD 'should be structured within a national framework in which all provision is accredited.' Sutherland acknowledged that in Scotland, CPD was already recognised as being important 'in strengthening the professional role of teachers.' As early as 1979, the *Green Report* had established a modular structure for award-bearing courses based on the principle of credit accumulation and transfer. There was controversy about the level of these courses. Hartley (1985) was critical of the fact that Level 1 of such courses often implied that teachers were technicians, learning how to do things and not being encouraged to be critical of national developments.

In 1998, SEED responded to Sutherland by publishing a consultation paper, *Proposals for developing a framework of continuing professional development for the teaching profession in Scotland.* It outlined a series of advantages of such a framework and suggested it would help Local Authorities in allocating resources.

> When teachers are better prepared the quality of teaching and learning improves, with a consequent benefit to pupil attainment and enhanced job satisfaction;
>
> When teachers are planning how to develop their careers the framework would serve as a guide to what development and training would be appropriate;
>
> Statements of competences and standards, derived with the support of the profession, should help to ensure that development and training are clearly related and effectively targeted the skills and knowledge teachers require; and
>
> The framework could help schools and education authorities to ensure that they have teachers with knowledge appropriate to their needs.
>
> (Kirk *et al.* 2003: pp. 3–4)

In 1992, a set of competences for initial teacher education had been produced. This 'standard' was an important part of the jigsaw. By 1998, there was also a Standard for Headship in Scotland which also set out the competences which would form the basis of the Scottish Qualification for Headship, introduced in 1999. To complete the picture, two further standards were necessary. The standard for full registration with GTCS was a set of competences to be expected of good classroom teachers. The final piece was the standard to which very good classroom teachers should aim. These were the building blocks of a national CPD framework. SEED put the contract for the development of the framework out to tender and it was won by the universities of Strathclyde and Glasgow working in partnership with Arthur Andersen management consultants. Quite why management consultants, earning the lion's share of the contract, were deemed to be necessary, remains unclear. Perhaps, it was felt that the private sector somehow gave a 'harder edge' to the eventual framework?

It was the McCrone Report, *A Teaching Profession for the 21st Century*, which finally made the case for Chartered Teacher. The programme was described as 'an alternative route for experienced classroom teachers who wished to develop their professional expertise within the classroom, rather than seeking promotion to a management post.' In itself, this idea, as we have seen, was unremarkable, but it did reveal an interesting misunderstanding of the role of Senior Teacher and even Principal Teacher.

Senior Teacher was not a 'management post'. It had been introduced as a consequence of the previous teacher settlement and was, in the first instance, a post which recognised the contribution of experienced teachers. In the event, because of local agreements between local employers and teaching unions, these posts became open to almost all teachers and began to attract a range of duties, not normally managerial, but certainly, in many cases cross-curricular. In other words, it became a new 'first step' on the promotion ladder.

Principal Teacher, on the other hand, was an established post in the secondary school structure, but not in primary schools. Traditionally a Principal Teacher ran a subject department, or more than one. In the late 1960s, it was not uncommon for a Principal Teacher to be responsible for all of the sciences, biology, physics and chemistry, or even such combinations as english, history and geography. This was a time of teacher shortages and a recruitment drive saw the creation of a career structure which not only saw the creation of PT posts for each individual subject (with some exceptions such as the modern languages or technical subjects such as woodwork and metalwork), but also saw the introduction of the Guidance system, which saw the creation of APT, PT and AHT posts.

However, neither ST nor PT was ever a truly 'management' post. PT did involve some managerial duties, mostly of an administrative nature, but it was essentially a leadership role. The role of subject leader in the secondary school was the 'engine room' of the school, the locus of curricular change and the arena in which learning and teaching policies where turned into practice in the classroom. Certainly, the PT was expected to 'manage' change, usually with little or no management training, and could be held to account by the Senior Management Team for any failures of her/his department, for example in terms of examination results, but these management duties were always a minor part of the role. After all, the title was Principal *Teacher*, and, at most, the post-holder was given an additional allocation of time amounting to around a quarter of the teaching for management. The PT was still, quite clearly, a teacher.

The key difference which Chartered Teacher was to herald was that it was to be a 'grade' not a 'post'. No management duties of any kind were to be taken on and the key task of any CT was to 'to play a significant role in promoting standards of excellence in teaching'. It was envisaged that the CTs would have some influence on their colleagues and would become a 'resource for the nation as well as for their schools and Local Authorities.' It was difficult to see how these roles could be overtaken by any CT simply by working effectively with pupils in classrooms. How would this 'influence on colleagues' be exerted? Would there be observation of lessons, participation in CPD, involvement in working groups? And exactly what did the term 'resource' mean? How would the resource be deployed? What call on CTs would the Local Authority and the nation have? How would the schools use this resource? These questions remained unanswered in the Report, but there followed an Agreement, reached by an Implementation Group, and the details of the Chartered Teacher concept began to emerge.

Kirk *et al.* (2003) describe the 'extensive consultation' which took place with the teaching profession in the wake of the Agreement. Interestingly, however, no figures are provided on the numbers of teachers who responded. Instead, broad conclusions are drawn from the exercise, including a long list of qualities suggested for a Chartered Teacher; endorsement of the Modular programme structure (four for Certificate; eight for Diploma; twelve for Masters); insistence that the assessment regime should be a balance of the practical and the theoretical; and agreement on the nature of the four core Modules (self-evaluation; learning and teaching; education for all; and working together).

A second consultation paper was issued on the Standard for Chartered Teacher. Again, no figures are provided for the responses, but the 'remarkable degree of consensus' is indicated by the percentages of responses to each question. What emerged was a 'Standard based on Professional Commitments, Professional Knowledge; Professional and Personal Attributes and Professional Action' supported by 90 per cent of respondents. A number of the elements of these four dimensions had a specific emphasis on CPD.

The second of the Commitments concerned 'self-critical evaluation and development'. This might include engaging with others, reading about teaching, undertaking research as part of 'the search for new and improved ways of supporting pupils' learning. The third commitment was to collaboration and centred on the 'impact' of the Chartered Teacher on the practice of others. Specific reference was made to CPD as a vehicle for this impact.

In the Professional Knowledge and Understanding dimension, an emphasis was placed on the expectation that Chartered Teachers would have a wide knowledge of theory, of the social context of education and of ethics. All of this would require a commitment to reading widely, to debating important issues and to engaging with a range of other stakeholders in the education process.

The issue of Attributes, always problematic in terms of their susceptibility to change, was couched in positive psychological and cultural terms. The word 'smeddum' is coined by Kirk and his colleagues to encapsulate diligence, determined and optimistic. They argue that the attributes of the good professional vary little from profession to profession.

Finally, Professional Action is couched in terms of 'performance' and there is specific reference to CPD, 'to improve professional performance (for example, by engaging in targeted CPD, or by adopting innovative approaches)' (Kirk *et al.* 2003: p. 21).

It is clear that from the outset, CPD was regarded as a central component of the Chartered Teacher programme. Put crudely, a teacher cannot become Chartered except through an extensive programme of CPD at postgraduate level. When Chartered status has been achieved, there is clearly an expectation that there will be a commitment to an involvement in, and contribution to, CPD throughout the rest of a Chartered Teacher's career.

Quoted in the *TESS* (May 2004) the recently appointed national CPD co-ordinator expressed some disappointment at the fact that only 6500 teachers had embarked on the Chartered

Teacher programme. This represents some 10 per cent of the profession and it is difficult to see how this could have been exceeded given the cost to each participant in terms of cash and time. The key challenge may not be how to increase the numbers following the Chartered Teacher route but rather the contribution they will make to learning and teaching once they have successfully completed the programme. Will they be content, metaphorically, to close their classroom doors and be excellent teachers or will they wish to contribute more widely to the promotion of excellence within their establishments or even within their authorities?

Taking the management route

Traditionally, the management route was the only route to take. If a teacher were to aspire to career advancement, it meant taking on a series of promoted posts. The concept of promotion is one which is not a feature of all educational systems. Essentially it means that teachers reach a point in their career development when they feel that they can move on to the next level of promotion. They apply for the post, take part in a competitive interview, have references written for them and a decision is made. If successful, the teacher takes up the new post, normally after two to three months, in the school where the post was vacant. There is little or no induction. The new recruit has moved into a management role, normally with no management training. It is the first rung on a management ladder, leading to headteacher and beyond.

So what are the implications? Well, for the individual teacher, it means the skills which made her a good teacher are unlikely to be those required in a good manager or leader. Not only that, the time given for management duties is derisory. Unlike the factory where a move from the shop-floor to the office means no more manual labour, in a school, the first management post means that the individual still teaches for the majority of the week. Time for management duties may add up to only a few hours, at most, and most tasks tend to be done in the teacher's own time. In the real world of a school, particularly a secondary school, pupil indiscipline is a key factor and very time consuming.

A lot of the administrative tasks are low-level, capable of being carried out by support staff. But they tend to be done at home. The key interface is the stage or departmental meeting, and these can often be ineffectual. The role of chair is a subtle one, but it is often carried out in a routine manner with little consideration of how meetings work dynamically. Much of the business is routine and the CPD element of these meetings is often low. In addition, the key role of monitoring and evaluation is often conspicuous by its absence.

Instead, heads of stage or department specialise in the 'maintenance agenda'. Development work is not a major feature of these groupings. Few unpromoted teachers are ever asked to lead sessions. Heads or Principal Teachers tend to dominate these meetings and they are concerned overwhelmingly with routine matters. Administration, 'housekeeping', record-keeping, responding to consultation documents from the senior management team, preparation of tests or exams papers, moderation of marking, and so on. For many heads of department these duties are a chore, often detracting from the developmental work they want to do. In recent years the time for such meetings has been eroded. In the secondary school, strong arguments were made in the 1980s that all departments needed an hour-long meeting each week during the school day if they were to manage the curricular changes taking place. When Planned Activity Time was introduced as part of an agreement on terms and conditions, compelling teachers to spend a given number of hours after school on a range of activities (one to one-and-a-half hours per fortnight, typically), many heads were encouraged to move departmental meetings into PAT. Now, in the immediate post-McCrone era, they tend to have moved back into the school day but normally on a once-a-fortnight basis.

The result is that the CPD element of departmental meetings has been further eroded. The likelihood is that CPD at a departmental level now probably only happens during in-service days. Theoretically, the 35 hours CPD time which is now every teacher's entitlement could take place as a department at meetings arranged outside of the school day for that purpose. Then it might be possible for these to take the form of workshops, lead by any member of the department or even by an external tutor, but there is no way of ensuring that all staff would be willing to use their 35 hours in this collegiate way.

The role of the Principal Teacher, while it does not mean departing the classroom entirely, carries with it enough administrative burdens to make it unattractive to many teachers who want to focus on classroom teaching. This is magnified ten-fold when the move from Principal Teacher to Depute is made. In an increasing number of schools this means either no class commitment at all or a much reduced involvement in class teaching. It might still include taking classes to relieve colleagues, taking a single class or maybe two in the secondary school, or it might involve taking SE classes, doing co-operative teaching or even learning or behaviour support. The bulk of the week is spent on administration, on crisis-management, on discipline-related work or in meetings. It can result in a distorted view of the school: no live teaching experience, dealing with pupils mainly because they are in trouble or are in some difficulty, meeting with external agencies and contacting parents whose children are in some kind of situation which requires their involvement. It can be developmental too: providing the stimulus or support or resources for others to develop new ideas, new methods and new initiatives, can be very rewarding; being there for staff and pupils who need someone to listen or to mediate or to give advice may be a central source of satisfaction. But it is often a far cry from the skills and attributes which made the individual a successful teacher in the first instance.

Scottish Qualification for Headship

The early thinking in *A Framework for Leadership and Management Development in Scottish Schools* (1997) was couched in language which is reflected in the later Chartered Teacher literature. It described three elements in its model:

- The professional qualities behind an act.
- The management functions which are the action.
- The personal abilities displayed in undertaking the act.

(SEED 1997: p. 9)

Emerging from the model was a set of school leadership and management competences which, in turn were expressed in terms of Key Tasks. Under the heading 'Develop teams, individuals and self to enhance performance' were the following tasks:

- Agree and support professional development targets for individuals and working groups.
- Monitor, evaluate and improve the professional development of individuals and working groups.

- Establish participative management structures.
- Develop oneself within the job role.

(SEED 1997: p. 22)

There was a section in the document headed 'Using the Framework to support Professional Development' which included exemplars on how it might be used in a variety of school contexts. Finally, in the Summary, the way was prepared for 'the possibility of qualifications in school leadership and management to be developed nationally' (1997: p. 41).

The developments which have taken place since 1997 have been rapid. The Scottish Qualification for Headship is well established and there have been 'graduation' ceremonies, attended by the Minister for Education. The LAMPS programme has been established and the situation has been reached that everyone who aspires to any senior management post within a school will have to undertake SQH, and will, almost certainly, have demonstrated a commitment to CPD through one or more of the other routes previously.

Thirty-five hours CPD – entitlement or obligation?

Douglas Blane's feature in the *Times Educational Supplement Scotland* (March 2004) entitled 'Keep learning and up to date' identified 'attitude to change' as a key defining characteristic of the modern teacher. While 'I wish they'd leave us alone to get on with the job' was once the prevailing attitude, now, newly qualified teachers are emerging from Initial Teacher Education with a 'willingness to change', according to Tom Fleming, headteacher of St Andrew's Primary School in Cumbernauld. The *TESS* article featured five teachers, ranging in experience from 5 to 30 years, and examined how the new probationary year was working and how the 35 hours CPD was impacting on the professional practice of more experienced teachers.

The least experienced of the five teachers reinforced the view often expressed in schools that having a probationer teacher or a student in the classroom was itself a powerful form of CPD. His Local Authority offered a range of CPD activities and his particular interest was in ICT. Already he had started working towards the European Computer Driving Licence, was exploring PowerPoint and the Smartboard for use in his classroom. His experience of pupils with additional support needs had led him to do some reading about specific conditions, and his comment that 'it is good to know that kind of thing – professional reading – is valued', underlines the new wider definition of CPD being applied in schools, post-McCrone. His CPD folder was being maintained and the Chartered Teacher programme was his next goal.

However, his colleague of 30-years experience expressed no particular interest in the Chartered Teacher programme. His feeling was that most teachers are professional and committed and keen to 'talk about education and teaching strategies'. His belief was that teachers are 'more in touch with change nowadays and know they have to keep up to date.' This sentiment was echoed by his colleagues of ten, fourteen and fifteen years experience respectively. They talked of keeping everything they did in terms of CPD 'in a box' for future reference and as evidence. They kept diaries, self-evaluated and ensured their portfolio was up to date. The authority had embarked on a programme of CPD around Co-operative Learning, and some of the staff had been attending twilight session and even a summer school. Some of the staff saw the Chartered Teacher programme as being too much of a challenge, both in terms of time and financially. Another had embarked on the Scottish Qualification for Headship, which included compiling a substantial portfolio which 'certainly makes you more reflective.'

Douglas Blane's snapshot of staff in one Authority suggested that the 35 hours CPD, now a condition of service, has 'played its role in altering attitudes to change'. Simply keeping a record makes a difference, according to a secondary teacher, and 'makes you feel that bit more professional.' A secondary depute headteacher observed that 'stagnation is no longer an option for anybody. Anyone who isn't open to all the opportunities for professional development these days will get left behind.'

CPD – half empty or half full?

If the *TESS* article has painted a picture of typical teachers in a typical Authority, it would appear that the CPD revolution has indeed begun. It is difficult not to agree with the claim that the more CPD there is in the system the better it is for teachers, pupils and schools in general. But there are doubts which remain. Does more CPD make you a better teacher, leader or manager, necessarily? Are the present models of CPD robust and well evaluated? Is there capacity in the system to satisfy the demand for high quality CPD? Will the outcomes, now, more than ever, expressed in terms of postgraduate qualifications, be valued by the profession and by the recipients of the education process? And if the claim that we are moving inexorably not just to a Masters profession but to a Doctoral profession, what are the implications for current notions of what makes a 'good teacher'?

The positive angle on this is that in the next decade or so all teachers will have the opportunity to be reflective about their own practice, will work in more collegiate ways, will subject theory and research to a rigorous critique and will understand more about the process of learning and how they can promote it effectively for *all* learners. The more sceptical perspective might be that so much attention being paid to counting the hours spent in CPD, gathering 'evidence', writing essays for Chartered Teacher or Scottish Qualification for Headship, might actually detract from the 'core business' of learning and teaching. The early euphoria of access to CPD and the recognition of reflection as a legitimate professional activity, may wane as some staff pursue Chartered Teacher and earn significant additional salary, while others, equally hard-working and professional and equally effective in the classroom, may not because of time or cost constraints. The early signs are mixed; positive attitudes to CPD but a slow uptake of the Chartered Teacher programme. Time alone will tell.

In the next chapter we will consider how CPD can contribute to the effectiveness of schools and of the cluster of schools. We will look at what research is telling us about the role of CPD and ask if there is any evidence that a teacher/school which invests in CPD actually improves learning and teaching. Finally we try to establish what pupils think about teachers' professional development.

SUMMARY

A Teaching Profession for the 21st Century signalled a new status and role for CPD. The probationary period has been transformed. Not only is it now one year rather than two, but probationary teachers are now counted as only 0.7 (FTE) in the staffing complement of the establishment, with the remaining 0.3 as an entitlement to high quality CPD. The Chartered Teacher post is a creation of the *McCrone Report* and is still in its infancy. As an attempt to provide an alternative career path for teachers, one which does not involve managerial responsibility, Chartered Teacher is likely to have more success than the ill-fated Senior Teacher post introduced in the early 1990s. Chartered Teachers will have successfully gained a postgraduate qualification (at their own expense) at Masters level with an emphasis on work-based learning. At the same time, the Scottish Qualification for Headship must now be achieved by anyone aspiring to become a headteacher in an attempt to ensure that there is a baseline standard of knowledge, skills and values at senior management level. Finally, the 35 hours CPD annually for all teachers can be seen as an entitlement or as an imposition, something which liberates and enriches teachers or something which forces them to undertake activities against their will or even to pay lip service to the concept of CPD.

POINTS FOR REFLECTION

1. Are the new arrangements for CPD in the Probationary year likely to form the foundation for a more reflective profession?

2. Is it true to say that the traditional promoted posts were 'management' posts?

3. What are your views of the Chartered Teacher concept, in theory and in practice?

4. Will SQH improve the quality of leadership and management in headteachers?

7 Ask not what CPD can do for you...!

> 'I'm still here,' said Piglet.
> 'Oh – so you are.'
> I enjoyed the stories.'
> 'That's good.'
> 'They helped me to... reflect on things.'
> 'Things? Such as –'
> 'Fear'
> 'Oh.'
> 'Well, I'm going out on a walk, to do some thinking. I'll be back in a bit.'
> 'Right you are. Have a pleasant time.'
>
> *Winne the Pooh*, **A. A. Milne**

Reflection – with a little help from your friend?

Hopkins and Lagerweij (1996) have attempted to characterise decades of approaches to educational improvement in the UK: the 1960s was the decade of curriculum development and the production of materials to improve classroom practice; the 1970s was revisionist and rejected much of this approach; in the 1980s, the school effectiveness movement identified key factors in successful schools; the 1990s moved on to school improvement. Now in the early part of the twenty-first century, CPD appears to the key element of the strategy. This picture may be true of England and Wales but the only point of reference with Scotland is the twenty-first century. The 1960s in Scotland saw a new Examination Board, a new General Teaching Council and a constituted Consultative Council on the Curriculum, and therefore the key issues were to do with structures and certification. It was in the 1970s, the decade of the Reports, that the production of curriculum materials became the main instrument of improvement. This continued into the 1980s, delayed, crucially by teacher industrial action, leading to even greater central control, stopping short of a statutory national curriculum but having a similar impact on schools. It was the late 1980s and the 1990s which saw the school effectiveness movement take hold in the shape of the Audit Unit of HMI and its production of sets of Indicators on ethos, performance, exam results and attendance. Form the late 1990s onwards, now given impetus by the *McCrone Report*, CPD has been seen by policy-makers as being central to the improvement process.

Adey (2004) has argued that the contribution which CPD can make to the development of the individual teacher, the classroom and the school has to be more than simply reflection. It must be about changes in practice. The theory is that a more reflective profession will become a more effective profession. Teachers who think together, share good practice and work together towards whole-school improvement will be teachers who are committed to CPD. This argument is very persuasive, but what is the evidence so support it? School effectiveness research is around 40-years old, and there is, therefore, a substantial body of evidence to indicate what the characteristics of effective schools are. The question is, where does CPD fit in? Does CPD make teachers and the schools in which they work more effective?

The literature suggests that it does. Since Michael Rutter and his colleagues changed forever the face of school effectiveness research with their book *Fifteen Thousand Hours* (1979), the race has been on to identify the characteristics of an effective school. Rutter identified 'ethos' as a key issue, defined as the quality of relationships in a school. However, these relationships are not forged and maintained by accident. Schools need to work at them, and one way of doing so is through CPD. Michael Fullan (1992: p. 114) has argued that 'teacher development and school development must go hand in hand'. Fullan begins by looking at initial teacher education and cites a study by Goodlad from 1990 which identified four sets of expectations for teacher education programmes:

1 That they will prepare teachers to enculturate the young into a political democracy.
2 That they will provide teachers with the necessary intellectual tools and subject-matter knowledge.

3 That they will ensure that teachers have a solid initial grounding in pedagogy.

4 That they will develop in teachers the beginning levels of the knowledge and skills required to run our schools.

(1992: p. 699)

In this American study, the authors found that most of the programmes they studied fell short of these expectations. Firstly, there were few opportunities for the student teachers to interact in relation to their experiences in school placements, other than in formal classes. There was little conscious preparation for the collegiality which is seen as a necessary part of school improvement. Secondly, in universities, where initial teacher education takes place, there had been an emphasis on research rather than teaching and lecturers were experiencing 'status deprivation' as a consequence. Thirdly, the focus in most teacher education programmes was on the classroom, rather than the school, and as a result, the experience of the student teachers was often disjointed. Finally, courses in educational philosophy and the social foundations of education had been seriously eroded.

It is true that since the early 1990s, there has been considerable change in initial teacher education in Scotland. True, it has now been located within Universities across the whole of the country, and some of the tensions Goodlad identified, particularly the research vs. teaching issue, have surfaced here too. There have been attempts to look at the whole school in the form of elements entitled 'Contexts' or 'Principles', but, paradoxically, these are not always highly rated by students in their course evaluations. Perhaps the finding which resonates most with the Scottish system is the lack of collegiality in the structure of the initial teacher education courses. This is most obvious between courses, so that on one campus there might be students following the four-year B.Ed. (Primary) course, the one-year PGCE (Primary) course, the one-year PGCE (Secondary) course (not to mention, courses in speech therapy, social work, community education, sports science, and so on). The opportunities for collegiality are minimal.

Fullan observes that since the mid-1980s, there have been some studies which have shown evidence of collegial and collaborative approaches to school improvement. Rosenholtz (1989) developed the notion of the 'moving' school. In such schools, she found evidence of collaboration being linked to 'opportunities for improvement and career-long learning'. Her conclusion that it is 'far easier to learn to teach, and to learn to teach better, in some schools than others' (p. 104) highlights the link between CPD and school improvement. She develops this point further:

> Where teachers request from and offer technical assistance to each other, and where school staff enforces consistent standards for student behaviour, teachers tend to complain less about students and parents. Further, where teachers collaborate, where they keep parents involved and informed about their children's progress, where teachers and principal work together consistently to enforce standards for student behaviour, and where teachers celebrate their achievements through positive feedback from students, parents, principal, colleagues, and their own sense, they collectively tend to believe in a technical culture and their instructional practice.
>
> (1989: p. 137)

Fullan warns against what he calls 'superficial and contrived forms of collegiality' and suggests that what schools need is 'learning and improvement on the part of teachers to become habitual' (1992: p. 117).

Personal, professional and institutional improvement – a balancing act?

Fullan's definition of staff development as including 'any activity or process intended to enhance skills, attitudes, understandings or performance in present or future roles' (1992: p. 97) emphasises its potential effect on the individual. Much of the research into school effectiveness has emphasised the link between staff development and effective innovations (Fullan and Pomfret, 1977). It is this link between the development of the individual and the management of the improvement process at an institutional level which has been the subject of much research attention in recent years. Conlon (2004) has argued, in the context of New Opportunities Fund (NOF) training for teachers on the use of new technology in the classroom, such training will only support and help bring about change in teacher practice if certain elements are in place. He offers a conceptual framework against which such training should be evaluated and finds NOF training wanting.

Impact on practice

Value congruence   Knowledge and skills

Motivation   Affective   Institutional

Provisionary   Information   Awareness

(p. 132)

Conlon's 'hierarchy of outcomes' is based on Harland and Kinder's categorisation of the possible outcomes of CPD:

- *Material and provisionary* outcomes are the physical resources which result from participation in CPD activities, such as worksheets, equipment and time.
- *Informational* outcomes refer to briefings concerning background facts and developments.
- *New awareness* is a shift in assumptions about what constitutes the appropriate content and delivery of a particular curriculum area.
- *Value congruence* refers to the degree of harmony that exists between the CPD participant's individual 'code of practice' and the CPD providers' messages about practice.
- *Affective* outcomes are the emotional changes, such as elation or demoralisation, that may follow from a CPD experience.
- *Motivational and attitudinal* outcomes refer to the enhanced enthusiasm and motivation to implement ideas derived from CPD.
- *Knowledge and skills* refer to the acquisition of new understandings or knowledge relating to curriculum content or pedagogy.
- *Institutional* outcomes describe the collective impact upon groups of teachers and their practice.
- *Impact on practice* denotes change in classroom repertoire or other forms of changes in professional practice brought about via the outcomes listed above.

Conlon's trenchant criticism of the NOF training identifies a number of deficiencies (underlined in the diagram above) when Harland and Kinder's categories are applied. He concludes that teachers' practice was not much changed by the training and that the impact on pupils' learning was minimal. He is critical of the 'delivery' (or 'Postman Pat') model of CPD and of the 'market' approach.

Fullan argues that staff development 'should be innovation-related, during the course of implementation and involve a variety of formal (e.g. workshops) and informal (e.g. teacher-exchange) components' (1992: p. 98). Indeed, in his latest work (2003) he suggests that the traditional balance of centrally provided and school-generated staff development should be reversed, and that schools should exploit the talent and expertise within their own staff much more than at present.

Stallings (1989) has outlined a number of conditions under which teachers are more likely to change their behaviours or to use new ideas:

1 They become aware of a need for improvement through their analysis of their own observation profile.
2 They make a written commitment to try new ideas in their classroom the next day.
3 They modify the workshop ideas to work in their classroom and school.
4 They try the ideas and evaluate the effect.
5 They observe each other's classrooms and analyse their own data.
6 They report their success or failure to their group.
7 They discuss problems and solutions regarding individual students and/or teaching subject matter.
8 They need a wide variety of approaches; modelling, simulations, observations, critiquing video tapes, presenting at professional meetings.
9 They learn in their own way continuity to set new goals for professional growth.

(1989: pp. 3–4)

This picture of professional development will be familiar to some schools but quite challenging to most. The primary school in Scottish Borders Council which, in the early 1990s, worked collaboratively to introduce new approaches to learning and teaching, engaged in 'focused monitoring' and encouraged the newly qualified teachers to take the lead in new developments, was fulfilling many of Stallings' conditions. The secondary school in which a number of staff had begun using video to analyse one another's practice and had freed up the members of the group to 'shadow' classes looking at specific aspects of pupil learning and feeding back their analysis to colleagues, was also fulfilling most of the conditions. However, there are still many schools where these practices do not take place. How, then, can CPD begin to move beyond its traditional models to incorporate aspects of the Stallings model, a model tried and evaluated empirically with impressive evidence of improvements in student attainment?

Application of the model to Scottish education

They become aware of a need for improvement through their analysis of their own observation profile

Since the *McCrone Report*, teachers have had to maintain a CPD profile. Many schools, some of which had been moving in this direction anyway, saw the opportunity to redefine the range of activities which constitute CPD. Classroom observation came to be seen not as a threat, as it had been perceived when it was associated with 'appraisal', but as a key aspect of the school improvement process. Local Authorities produced guidance on the issue, apprehensive, perhaps, of how such observation could be counterproductive if badly handled within a school, especially if staff were not fully involved in the discussions which should precede any such approach. Observing oneself teaching has always been problematic (Brown, 1989) and there is no doubt that a trusted and non-threatening colleague, for most teachers, is more likely to be conducive to self-analysis than a member of the senior management team, or a member of Her Majesty's Inspectorate.

They make a written commitment to try new ideas in their classroom the next day

The issue of written commitments would be problematic in many schools and the pledge to try new ideas in the classroom *the next day* might be difficult to fulfil if the curriculum is not flexible enough to allow it to happen. Indeed, the issue of putting something on paper after observational visits have taken place has, for come schools, itself been a stumbling block. Where schools have successfully introduced peer observation as a process, they have spent a lot of time on Fullan's initiation stage, enabling staff to clarify the purpose of the observation, the focus of the visits, the way in which the resultant discussion will be structured and the nature and purpose of the notes that are made by both parties after the event.

They modify the workshop ideas to work in their classroom and school

What is clear is that the experience of observing and being observed should lead to changes in practice in due course, both for the individuals concerned and for their colleagues across the school. It is also true that CPD should have a similar impact. If a school devotes a day to exploring aspects of learning and teaching as part of its INSET programme, particularly if it has been done on a whole-school basis with cross curricular/cross stage groups discussing generic aspects of effective learning and teaching, then there should be discussion, later, within departmental/stage groupings as to how the ideas discussed in the CPD workshops could be put into practice in classrooms. Ideally, as part of the workshops, there should be discussion of the impediments to implementing any of these new ideas and a commitment on the part of the senior management team and others to try to remove these impediments so that the ideas can be tried.

They try the ideas and evaluate the effect

The trying of the ideas, equivalent to Fullan's implementation phase, may take some time. Indeed, it is often the case that insufficient time for the ideas to be tried fully is allowed, and initiatives simply run out of steam because of lack of support. If we accept that there are no 'quick fixes' in terms of improving learning and teaching, then new ideas are likely to require time to have an effect. Evaluation of these new ideas is crucial if any rational discussion of their impact is to take place. It is often the case that evaluation is not carried out when new ideas are implemented, whether in school or at national level. The reasons vary from a lack of time in the system for rigorous and systematic evaluation, to a lack of confidence in the process of evaluation itself. Occasionally, an external *critical friend* may be available to help with the evaluation, providing advice on instruments, qualitative and quantitative, observing classroom practice, interviewing stakeholders. But the key to successful management of change at school level must, ultimately, lie with staff becoming *au fait* with the process of evaluation and becoming confident about using a range of approaches to suit the situation.

They observe each other's classrooms and analyse their own data

There is an issue about who should do the observing. If you look at HMIE reports on schools, there is a clear expectation that observation is clearly connected with monitoring and evaluation and should be done by senior managers and heads of department. However, this kind of classroom observation is developmental. The parallel is with assessment. The Assessment is for Learning programme is clear that *formative* assessment should predominate in the teaching and learning process because it is about feedback to the learner to enable her/him to learn more effectively next time. On the other hand, *summative* assessment is about making judgements about progress to date. It tells us what the learner may be able to do now but not necessarily what he or she needs to do to improve. Peer observation is developmental and forward looking; observation which lies within the monitoring and evaluation sphere may only focus on what is happening now, as judged against quality indicators, for example, but may not be helpful to the person observed in terms of improvement.

They report their success or failure to their group

This may be more or less difficult depending on the culture of the school. Some schools have an open, participatory, collaborative culture in which it is accepted as the norm that teachers and those who work with them share their successes and their failures. In educational establishments other than schools, notably pre-5, the adults who work with children have established just such a culture. It can often be found, too, in primary schools, where all staff regularly meet together to discuss learning and teaching and where sharing successes and failures is commonplace. It is much less common in secondary schools, partly as a consequence of the departmental structure. 'Boundary maintenance' is strong within secondary schools, and opportunities for the whole staff to get together to discuss common issues such as learning and teaching may be few and far between. Within departments, it may be the case that such a culture exists. Departmental meetings may be developmental rather than administrative and bureaucratic; teachers may work together in teams to prepare new resources and approaches; classroom observation may be the norm; and it may be such a supportive atmosphere that staff are happy to share failures as well as successes. The challenge for secondary schools is to extend that collegiality across the whole staff and where it has been done, as in St Modan's High School in Stirling, it is spectacularly successful, as its HMIE report attests.

They discuss problems and solutions regarding individual students and/or teaching subject matter

The challenge for schools is to put learning and teaching at the heart of the matter. Open discussion of problems, general and specific, with a clear focus on finding and sharing solutions, is a key indicator of a 'moving' school. It could be argued that in any establishment of any significant size, there will be people who have experience and expertise in almost all aspects of teaching. There are few wholly new ideas under the sun, and it is common to find that somewhere in the organisation, someone has developed strategies which are successful in enabling children to learn successfully. If we accept that the whole of the child's schooling should be more than the sum of its individual parts, then those engaged in the learning and teaching process need to share their expertise. In a cluster of schools – secondary, primary, pre-5 and special – it is not uncommon for there to be upwards of 200 staff with, in total, some 5000 years of experience and accumulated expertise. The problem is that it is not shared often enough.

They need a wide variety of approaches: modelling, simulations, observations, critiquing video tapes, presenting at professional meetings

The kinds of approaches an educational establishment decides to use may well depend on the circumstances and even the individual staff involved. In one secondary school in the former Grampian region in the 1990s, a small working group of staff, mainly unpromoted, embarked on classroom observation via pupil shadowing. They agreed with colleagues the focus of the observation and fed back general findings to the rest of the staff. Meanwhile, some of the group began to video one another's lessons and jointly critiqued them. A secondary school in Carlisle spent the first of two consecutive INSET days as a whole staff discussing effective learning and teaching. The next day, around ten staff, all volunteers, conducted 'sample' lessons for their colleagues, highlighting particular aspects of their practice which they felt might be of more general interest. Staff in other schools, often as a result of having been identified by HMIE or advisers or the headteacher, are invited to present their practice to other professionals beyond the school. Indeed, in the 1970s and 1980s, this was a key role of HMI, 'talent-spotting' and then 'showcasing' good practice at local and national conferences. Nowadays, it is more likely to happen at a cluster or Council level. This commitment to sharing is what Michael Fullan refers to as the 'moral dimension' of education.

They learn in their own way continuity to set new goals for professional growth

If such practices become part of 'the way we do things around here', the school is on its way to becoming a learning community. In Scotland, the introduction of the 35 hours per year CPD entitlement, the commitment to CPD in the Probationary year, the establishment of the Chartered Teacher programme and the Scottish Qualification for Headship, all add up to a level of continuity which has never existed previously. The scene is set for a level of professional growth in the system which may empower teachers rekindling in many of them the kind of enthusiasm for learning and teaching which brought them into the profession in the first place.

CPD – the pupil perspective

If, in the moving school, all staff are focused on improving learning and teaching, are they interested in what pupils think of what it takes to be a good teacher? Do pupils' views feature in CPD? We have seen in Chapter 5 that the research done by MacBeath and others (1996) suggests that pupils have some insightful things to say about what makes a good teacher. But, do schools ever systematically seek pupils' views and feed them into CPD?

Rudduck and her colleagues (1996) looked at the aims which most schools have but from the perspective of the pupil. They arrived at 6 principles:

> **Respect** for pupils as individuals and as a body occupying a significant position in the institution of the school.
> **Fairness** to all pupils irrespective of their class, gender, ethnicity or academic status.

Autonomy – not as an absolute but both as a right and a responsibility in relation to physical and social maturity.

Intellectual challenge that helps pupils to experience learning as a dynamic, engaging and empowering activity.

Social support in relation to both academic and emotional concerns.

Security in relation to both the physical setting of the school and in interpersonal (including anxiety about threats to pupils' self-esteem.

It is arguable whether a school could be truly said to be 'moving' if it did not take into account the views of the learners. If teachers are being encouraged to ask 'what makes a good teacher?', what would pupils make of the same question?

It could be argued that any group of teachers would come up with a list which is very similar to that produced by the pupils. There may be differences in language and perhaps more emphasis on traits than strategies or techniques. But the pupils, in general terms, are insightful, if blunt. They know what makes a good teacher and even in Year 2/3 they can zoom into the key issues.

The good teacher:
- is very clever
- doesn't shout
- helps you every day
- is not bossy
- has faith in you
- is funny
- is patient
- is good at work
- tells you clearly what to do
- helps you with mistakes
- makes you work
- helps you to read
- helps you with spelling
- has got courage.

Studies throughout the UK over the last twenty years have identified four key characteristics of good teachers, from the pupils' perspective.

The good teacher:
- creates a sense of order
- is approachable
- is fair
- has a sense of humour.

This should reassure staff and it has to be said that when pupils are made aware of the ground rules when discussing the qualities of teachers, namely no names and no gratuitous comments, there is rarely a problem. Pupils are more than capable of entering into such discussions, and offer insights which are illuminating as shown in these lists of characteristics of strict teachers.

Strict for you	Strict for themselves
• Makes you do it and do it well	• Makes you do it
• You do it because you know they care for you	• Makes you do it because they say so
• You respect them but you're not frightened	• Is strict for its own sake
• You don't want to disappoint them	• It is to control you not to help you
• You learn a lot more	• It is to make up for their disorganisation
• You make good progress	• It makes a tense atmosphere; you don't learn so well

The message from research, and in particular from listening to the voices of pupils, is that effective teachers are people who continue to learn and who listen to the views of others. If the learning school is one in which everyone, potentially, learns from everyone else, then CPD is clearly a vehicle for such learning. In the past, teachers learned on courses and in formal in-service contexts. Now, CPD is to be perceived as a process, ongoing from Initial Teacher Education through the probationary year to full registration with the GTCS onwards for the rest of the teacher's career. The career may take the individual through Chartered Teacher and/or through the managerial post within the system and may conclude with participation in the Scottish Qualification for Headship. It will be a journey supported at every stage by CPD.

SUMMARY

Collegiality in schools can either be real or contrived, but most writers on the subject argue that it is the most powerful way of supporting staff to support pupils. Indeed, self-evaluation, including teacher observation, is best done within a collegial climate.

There have been some trenchant criticisms of some national policy initiatives which have failed to meet the aspirations of teachers in terms of training. NOF training in ICT has been singled out by Conlon as having failed to take account of the key principles of successful CPD. Other writers have attempted to set out key characteristics of successful CPD. Once again, the pupil perspective on teachers' skills can be a positive contribution to the debate on improvement, or it can be perceived as a threat.

POINTS FOR REFLECTION

1. Does existing Initial Teacher Education meet Goodlad's four criteria?

2. Would you say that your school is a 'moving' school? What evidence would you use to support your view?

3. Conlon is very critical of NOF training. Do think the criteria he uses are appropriate? Can you think of any other training programmes, national or local, which would be judged successful against these criteria?

4. How would your school's approach to CPD rate against Stalling's checklist?

5. Do pupils have anything significant to say about the quality of learning and teaching in schools? How can their views be addressed within a CPD programme?

8 CPD – current practice

> 'Just how do you do it, Pooh?'
> 'Do what?' asked Pooh.
> 'Become so Effortless.'
> 'I don't do much of anything,' he said.
> 'But all those things of yours get done.'
> 'They just sort of happen,' he said.
>
> *Winne the Pooh*, A. A. Milne

What can 'good practice' tell us?

One of the things we know about success in education is that it almost never 'just sort of happens.' Most improvements in education happen because a lot of people put in a huge amount of work. The best athletes, leaders, teachers and learners do seem to make it look so 'effortless', but it is rarely the case. Those who are blessed with exceptional talent know that to be successful it has to be complemented by a lot of hard work. If genius is actually '99 per cent perspiration and 1 per cent inspiration', then roughly the same percentages apply when good practice in CPD emerges.

In this chapter we are going to look at three examples of good practice involving Local Authorities, each of which involves the participation of a range of organisations, people and establishments. The first involves the secondment of two staff to produce a Toolkit for teachers in the area of Learning and Teaching. The second is an Authority-wide commitment to providing CPD for every member of staff on Co-operative Learning. The third is a partnership between an organisation, *Tapestry*, and individual local authorities designed to promote creativity in learning and teaching.

Thinking Skills and Toolkits

In the early 1990s, a (Regional) Council was in the vanguard of developments in Thinking Skills. Building on work done to support courses in Philosophy, it funded the development of a double postgraduate Module on 'Learning and Teaching from a Thinking Skills Perspective' written with staff from the University of Strathclyde and validated by the University. Until the late 1990s, these Modules were delivered using a mix of face-to-face conferences involving a range of contributors such as Professor Robert Fisher, author of *Teaching Children to Think*. Groups of staff met in local communities and worked through the eight sessions contained within the double Module.

Post local government reorganisation, the Thinking Skills initiative continued, albeit on a smaller scale. In the meantime, national developments, particularly Assessment is for Learning, were launched, and the Council seconded two members of staff to develop a package of materials entitled a Teachers' Toolkit to support CPD.

It was soon apparent that there was a huge overlap between the principles which underpin Assessment is for Learning and Thinking Skills. They both emphasised the importance of sharing learning objectives with the pupils and making explicit the criteria for success. Collaborative learning was a feature of both, based as they were on a Vygotskian model of 'social constructivism'. The teacher had a central role in each, particularly with an emphasis on the kinds of questioning strategies s/he should employ, especially questions which promote thinking as opposed to the kind of 'guess-what's-in-the-teacher's-head' kind of approach so common in classrooms. Thinking time featured in both as did formative assessment, whether by the teacher, the peer group of the pupil herself or himself. In both, active and independent learning was a key objective.

In March 2004, the Council ran a one-day conference in which Thinking Skills and Assessment is for Learning were featured and the connections made. The Toolkit was presented in outline form and four of its 42 sections were described as exemplars. One exemplar was the section on Questioning. The quality of teacher questioning, the balance of open and closed questions, alternatives to the traditional 'hands up' approach to eliciting pupil answers, dealing with 'wrong' answers, strategies to promote pupil thinking and simple ideas such as the 'three-second delay' are all featured.

The aim of the Council is to make this Toolkit available to all staff, teaching as well as support staff, as part of CPD. The Toolkit is generic, cross-curricular and cross-sectoral, and is designed to be more than simply a 'ten handy hints' approach. There is reference to theory and research, there are links to other developments within Scottish education and there are prompts for discussion and activity among groups of staff within schools and clusters of schools.

In addition, there is support for small-scale action research projects. Staff are encouraged to apply for funding to try out ideas from the Toolkit, to monitor their progress and to evaluate their impact on pupil learning. These projects are then made public through a dedicated website and thus the sharing of good practice is supported. Encouragement is given to groups of staff within a cluster of schools to look at issues which are generic and which can inform practice in learning and teaching from early years to late secondary.

Co-operative Learning

Co-operative Learning is a Canadian approach which has been adopted by one Council as part of their strategy to raise attainment for all and to promote social inclusion. In the *Resource Booklet* which accompanies the training, Ward and Craigen outline the rationale for Co-operative Learning. They argue that traditional models where the teacher's role was 'to impart knowledge' and the pupil's was to be a 'passive receptor of knowledge' will not meet the needs of the twenty-first century world. They suggest that we need to establish school climates which 'promote mutually supportive social settings' and within these schools the aim should be to create classroom which are 'co-operative …environments'. The authors link the idea of co-operative learning to the growing pluralism in society and suggest that it will help promote tolerance, respect for others and a sense of belonging among all young people in the twenty-first century.

The *Co-operative Learning Resource Booklet* has a brief Introduction organised around a number of key questions:

- What is Co-operative Learning?
- Why use Co-operative Learning?
- What makes Co-operative Groups Work?

There is a short list of References, mainly to works of the authors of Co-operative Learning. However it also sets out five basis elements of Co-operative Learning:

1 Positive interdependence: one cannot succeed unless everyone succeeds.
2 Promotive interaction: students promote one another's success.
3 Individual and group accountability: groups are accountable as is each member of the group.
4 Teaching students the required interpersonal and small group skills: social skills for successful group interaction need to be taught.
5 Group processing: groups discuss how well they are doing and how they are maintaining effective working relationships.

The Council has an ambitious plan to have every teacher in due course trained in Co-operative Learning approaches. It is not to the exclusion of every other approach, but is complementary, so initiatives involving Tony Buzan (Mind Mapping), Geoff Moss (Behaviour Management) and others are also taking place.

A partnership approach

In the year 2000, a new organisation called *Tapestry* was born. It was the brainchild of a small number of educationists, including the present author, who saw the enthusiasm among the teaching profession and others involved in life-long learning, for new ways of thinking about learning. Building on successful conferences in the late 1990s on 'thinking skills', featuring the work of Robert Fisher, among others, *Tapestry* was formed to bring leading edge thinkers about learning to Scotland. The tapestry metaphor was to stress the idea that there are many threads in the learning process which, once interwoven, can help educators to develop the potential of all learners. *Tapestry*'s threads were:

• brain-based learning
• music and the mind
• health and well-being.

The aim of the organisation was to promote a holistic view of learning, or, as the 2000 HMI report suggested in its title, *Educating the Whole Child*. Thus to promote effective learning, teachers and others would benefit from knowing more about how the brain works, how music can help in the learning process and how the whole person, including the emotions, is involved when successful learning takes place.

Each strand had its key international figures. Brain-based learning was promoted, in different ways by Tony Buzan (Mind Mapping), Professor Howard Gardner (Multiple Intelligences) and Professor Reuven Feuerstein (Instrumental Enrichment). Music and the mind was led by Professors Nigel Osborne and Paul Robertson, while Health and Well-being was promoted by Leslie Kenton and Carla Hannaford, one of the originators of the Brain Gym movement.

Within two years of its establishment, *Tapestry* had formed partnerships with most of the major organisations and institutions involved in education. In addition, since its mission included life-long learning, family learning and learning in the community, it included bodies outside of the formal school/education sectors. Initially, the *Tapestry* Board included three of the major Initial Teacher Education universities, the Convention of Scottish Local Authorities (COSLA), the Association of Directors of Education Scotland (ADES), Learning and Teaching Scotland, the national curriculum body, Scottish Further Education Unit (SFEU). In due course, organisations such as the Royal Scottish National Orchestra, the Royal Scottish Academy of Music and Drama, Scottish Enterprise and the Scottish Council of Independent Schools joined the partnership.

The appeal of *Tapestry* was that it worked in partnership rather than in competition with the established organisations in Scotland. It provided a model of CPD which had at the apex the International Conferences involving leading edge thinkers. It followed these up with a series of Masterclasses on related themes led by established experts in the field. Locally delivered courses were available to those authorities which wanted them and there was the option of 'training-the-trainers'.

The Tapestry Pyramid

The rationale underpinning the *Tapestry* approach can be portrayed as a pyramid.

Conference

The Masterclasses

The training of the trainers

Development of local initiatives with seconded staff

Provision of postgraduate Modules for Chartered Teacher programme

Locally delivered CPD for frontline staff at school or cluster or authority level

Ongoing research and evaluation of the impact of these activities on the pupils' learning

Conference

The role of the Conference is to bring the 'big names' to Scotland from across the world and from Scotland itself. They are invited to discuss their theories and ideas with a range of people – professionals, parents and young people. This dialogue enables those working at the frontline with learners to interrogate the ideas (and the speakers) and, in many cases, to be inspired by their message. However, the so-called 'Hawthorn Effect' applies here too where any new initiative appears to work because of its novelty. Many people can leave a conference energised and inspired but when reality kicks in days and weeks later, they may feel ill-equipped to translate the new ideas into practice.

The Masterclasses

The Masterclasses are more intimate affairs with smaller numbers of participants and more time for discussion and workshop activities. The themes are those of the Conference but the leaders of the sessions are people who, while still eminent in their field, have more experience of working at Local Authority, school and classroom level. Thus, there may be as many as six or eight Masterclasses following on from a Conference, enabling participants to home in on specific strands of the overall theme.

Training the trainers

Where the conference has been held for a particular Local Authority, built into the package is a number of follow-up sessions held in that Authority for key staff, including advisory staff and school staff. These sessions are more intensive and seldom have more than 20 to 25 participants. The accent is on training so that, for example, a Tony Buzan conference will have enthused people and sparked their interest in how the brain learns, how the memory can be developed, how Mind Maps can enhance learning and how 'connectedness' and 'association' are key ideas in learning. These follow-up sessions can enable key staff to explore the rationale for these approaches, the strategies to promote them in classrooms, from pre-school to post-16, and can offer models for dissemination at a school or cluster level in the context of CPD.

Development of local initiatives

Some Local Authorities have used a Conference to launch or support a local initiative and have decided to pull together a Working Group to explore a specific implementation strategy. Thus one Authority is producing a multi-media Creativity Pack aimed at the transition period between primary and secondary school. Another is looking at the development of support activities and materials to promote Family Learning. A third is looking at how the work of Reuven Feuerstein can be introduced into mainstream schools. In some cases, the authority has seconded a member of staff to support this initiative, even when the production of a pack or of materials is not the focus. One authority has decided to provide INSET for all staff in every secondary school on new approaches to learning and teaching, and to then offer the support of the seconded person and the *Tapestry* organisation, to each school to develop its own improvement agenda.

Provision of postgraduate Modules

In the post-McCrone era, the provision of CPD which can not only enhance the professionalism of staff but can contribute to their career development, is essential. While not every teacher will wish to pursue the Chartered Teacher route, the Modules which support the programme can be adapted to meet the needs of all staff. Thus a single session of an eight-session Module, might meet the needs of a department or a school or a cluster in one in-service day. Other staff might want to undertake the whole Module but not to seek, at that point in time, accreditation (leaving open the option of accreditation of prior learning at some point in the future). Each Module might explore a relatively narrow aspect of the new thinking about learning, and might have specific relevance to a stage or sector of education. Importantly, it will enable the reflective professional to engage with theory and test its impact on practice.

Locally derived CPD

The delivery of local in-service can be led by staff who have been either seconded to work on an initiative or who have been on the training-of-trainers sessions. They may be led jointly by local staff and *Tapestry* staff. The participants may be the whole staff of a cluster – up to 250 people – or it may be a small group who have been given a task to do within the school or cluster. It may be one session, it might be a series of inputs. The key here is flexibility and customisation. In other words, the CPD provision is geared to the aims of the establishments and supports the priorities of their Development Plans. It takes a theme, explores its practical implementation and build on the good practice of people working at a local level. The model is collaborative and the rationale is based on the Vygotskyan theory of social constructivism. The teachers and others working with the learners share their insights, exchange ideas and develop their understanding of the new approaches by working together and reflecting on their practice.

Ongoing research and evaluation

At the base of the pyramid lies an aspect of CPD which has been neglected historically and that is engagement of teachers with the research and evaluation process. In the past, where research was done at all, it was generally carried out by career researchers, mainly from universities, who would use their skills and expertise, produce a report, and then move on to the next contract. Too often, the teachers were not active participants in the process and often felt that the researchers were almost parasitic in the way in which they used the teachers' work to promote their own academic advancement. Now, the model is more akin to a blend of teacher-led action research and conventional evaluation processes. The teachers, either as part of Chartered Teacher, or out of professional interest, take the lead in identifying the issues for research/evaluation, help to design the methods and instruments and are involved in the analysis of the findings. In the process they develop new skills and are able to apply these to their own practice and that of their organisation. Thus, self-evaluation, the cornerstone of school improvement, is sharpened and enhanced.

This pyramid, is, of necessity, an idealised version, and, in reality, there will be many variants of it to suit local circumstances. The key issues are collaboration, partnership and empowerment. The big ideas are out there, but no one idea has a monopoly of wisdom. As Howard Gardner said at the end of a two-day *Tapestry* Conference at which he, Tony Buzan, Carla Hannaford, Nigel Osborne, Ben Zander and Paul Robertson had spoken, 'if you (the audience) have agreed with everything you have heard over the last two days, then you haven't been listening.' There is no single right answer to the problem of underachievement in learning. There are many answers, and those involved in the learning process should be supported to apply those which best suit their circumstances.

Monitoring and evaluating CPD

How different a school would be without CPD is a difficult question to answer. Given the amount of money spent annually on CPD, it is important that the question be asked. It has been argued that the raising of CPD to the level of an entitlement of 35 hours per year per teacher has now made it a central plank of the school improvement agenda. When all the money spent nationally on CPD is considered, at school, Local Authority and national level, it amounts to a significant sum. Yet, many teachers each year cannot go on in-sevice courses, either because the school's budget is not sufficient or because there is a shortage of supply teachers to cover classes. So, how would we know whether there is too little, enough or too much CPD? How would such a question be answered? What criteria would be used and who would be best placed to evaluate its success?

Every in-service course which teachers attend nowadays has an evaluation form to be completed, normally before the session ends. What does the information gleaned from such forms tell us? Is such an on-the-spot approach to evaluation really the best way of judging the success of CPD? How is the impact of such experiences measured, on the teacher's thinking and behaviours; on pupils' experiences and attainment; on the overall effectiveness of the educational establishment? As we have seen, the assessment built into Chartered Teacher Modules emphasises the impact on professional practice. Can the same criterion be applied to CPD generally?

Guskey (2000) has argued that there are several different levels of evaluation of any professional development programmes. Level 1 is the end-of-session evaluation form which characterise most in-service events and which Guskey refers to as 'trivial'. The top level, he suggests, is the impact on students' achievement associated with the actions promoted by the professional development experience. However, Doyle (1977) has warned about 'the unwarranted assumption of causality' and suggests that there is more complex interrelationship between teacher interventions and pupil learning than some commentators have suggested.

If monitoring and evaluation is important, who is best placed to carry it out? The most obvious answer in most schools would be the staff development co-ordinator, normally a depute headteacher. This is the person in most schools who manages the CPD budget, to whom all information about courses is passed and whose responsibility it is to ensure that the lessons from CPD are disseminated to as many of the staff as possible. From a strategic perspective, the School Development Plan is the framework within which CPD is set. The aims of the SDP, theoretically a mix of national, council and school priorities, will almost certainly require staff to undertake CPD where new ideas, approaches or curriculum content are concerned. Against this, the need of the individual needs to be balanced. And, of course, the main beneficiary of all of this activity should be... the pupil.

The literature

Given the huge body of work over the last 30 years or so on school effectiveness and school improvement, and in particular the recognition of the importance of CPD, there is no shortage of advice on how monitoring and evaluation should be conducted. Hall and O'Connor suggest the following set of headings for a school policy on staff development:

- Induction of new recruits and the building of teams including new and existing staff.
- Induction for existing staff taking on new roles in school.
- Induction of volunteers/supply staff/regular visitors/new governors.
- Staff-development opportunities: individual and group events and courses, visits and observations, mentoring, on and off-site opportunities.
- Criteria for supporting staff development requests, linked to school priorities, personal career development, or both.

- Teaching and support staff appraisal, training and development.
- Monitoring and evaluation of staff development policy and practice at individual, team and whole school levels.

(Times Educational Supplement (TES): 1994)

Their view is that all staff should be involved in the improvement process since they are the school's most valuable resource. They make reference to Investors In People (IIP) which many schools have now applied for in an effort to achieve external recognition for the quality of their staff training and development. They go on to suggest a 'Checklist for quality staff development' which is derived from the IIP documentation and which should, for each school, be aligned with the School Development Plan.

Checklist for quality staff development:

- Is there a school development plan and is it reviewed at least annually?
- Does everyone who works at the school know the school aims and the priorities of the development plan?
- Does everyone know what is expected of them? Do they all have job descriptions?
- Are the head (and governors) committed to developing all the staff?
- Is there a staff development policy and does it include all staff, not just the teachers?
- Is there a staff development plan?
- Does it follow naturally from the school development plan?
- Do all staff have the opportunity to be appraised at least annually?
- Are responsibilities for training and development specified in job descriptions?
- Are managers competent to carry out their responsibilities for developing people?
- Are they appraised using agreed guidelines for the role of line managers?
- Are there induction programmes for new staff and for existing staff taking on new roles?
- Does everyone have a training and development plan and is it linked to school priorities?
- What are your attitudes to staff obtaining extra qualifications?
- Does the planned training and development actually happen?

- Are training and development events evaluated?
- Are the outcomes of training and development evaluated?
- Does the investment in training and development (both money and time) give value for money?
- Are the school's professional training days and other on-site development activities evaluated?
- Does the training and development as a whole help the school to achieve its objectives?
- What evidence and records do the senior managers provide (for the governors) when reporting the contribution of staff development programme at individual, team and whole school levels, to the school development plan?

(TESS: 1994)

Local Authority – supporting CPD in its schools?

One Local Authority, like many others, offers advice to its schools on CPD as part of the 'improvement agenda' via a document entitled, *Guidelines on Continuing Professional Development*. In 2001, the Council, under the joint signatures of the Executive Director, Education Resources and the Chair JCC (teachers' side), issued a document, *Guidelines on Continuing Professional Development*. Its rationale was that 'attitudes and capabilities of individual teachers and the culture in establishments make critical contributions to providing a world class education service' (2001: p. 5). CPD was seen as a 'bridge' between where the service was at any given point and where it needed to be to meet the challenges of the twenty-first century. The role of CPD was seen as pivotal and the description of a school which could be said to be a 'learning organisation' had CPD at its heart:

> An establishment in which teachers individually and collectively seek, and are supported to develop and extend their expertise is one that is likely to value professional growth. It is therefore possible to think of creating a climate within an establishment conducive to both individual and establishment development. The establishment with such a climate can be described as a learning organisation. Such an establishment is characterised by being interactive and negotiative, creative and responsive, challenging and supportive and evaluative and reflective. It is an establishment which both fosters and is a product of continuing professional development.

(2001: p. 5)

This Council is clearly positioning CPD as the focal point in 'the learning organisation'. It could be argued that these claims are too grandiose or that the learning organisation involves more than simply CPD, but there is no doubt that such a statement represents a powerful commitment on the part of the Council.

The document goes on to outline a set of principles of CPD, outlines key features and suggests a range of activities which count as CPD, including:

- Attendance at conferences and courses
- Development work
- Membership of working groups
- Self-directed study
- Secondments/acting posts
- Collaborative learning
- Research
- Staff development and review.

(2001)

It also lists the range of CPD opportunities which the Council offers, where and when it can be accessed and then proceeds to outline the roles and responsibilities of:

- the individual teacher
- the line manager
- the staff development co-ordinator
- the head of establishment
- the Council/Education Resources
- SEED.

(2001)

Finally, after a short section on Budgets, there is a detailed description of the Personal CPD Plan/Records with a Draft Exemplar (see Appendix).

All-in-all, the document, only eighteen pages long, and written in the formal style of a Council report, represents the clearest possible commitment to CPD in the context of school improvement. No school in this Authority can have any doubt about the view taken on the role of CPD and its importance in the improvement process.

The school

One school has produced a set of documentation to support its own CPD strategy, in the context of the Council guidelines. In its

Introduction to Continuing Professional Development, staff are led through a question-and-answer sequence laying out the key elements of the more formal, and lengthier, *Council Guidelines* (see Appendix).

In addition, there is diagrammatic representation of the role of CPD, summarising on one sheet of A4 the main body of content of the Council's Guidelines document. The sheet can be kept in the individual teacher's portfolio, pinned up in the Departmental Base or in the Staff Development Co-ordinator's room. It is an easy-to-understand visual guide to the key elements of the Council's strategy.

Perhaps the most substantial element of the school's documentation for staff is the four-page, A5 leaflet entitled *Opportunities for Staff Development* (see Appendix). Under nineteen categories there are some 90 or so examples of activities which could be regarded as CPD, from involvement in staff development and review to shadowing classes, from co-operative teaching to being a member of a working group, from taking part in in-service training to piloting new approaches to learning and teaching. The list is not exhaustive, but it certainly is impressive!

Finally, the in-school package includes a series of examples of completed Continuing Professional Development Plan/Record of the kind contained in the Council document (see Appendix). It takes three fictitious members of staff – a classroom teacher, an APT Guidance and a Principal Teacher – and shows what a completed Plan/Record might look like over a school session. The balance of activities is different in each case, outlining activities within and outwith the working (35 hour) week. The evaluation comments are brief but pertinent.

The documentation produced by the school is helpful and supportive. It is designed to enable all staff to find a balance of CPD activities which meets individual and school needs. If avoids the pitfall of over-elaborate bureaucracy and promotes in a low-key way a new way of looking at CPD.

 **SUMMARY**

The issue of 'good practice' can be problematic. Who defines 'good' and can practice be transferred to new situations or contexts? Local Authorities have chosen quite different approaches and have focused on different aspects of learning. Some have bought into existing programmes while others have seconded staff to provide support for teachers. Organisations have emerged which exist outside of the SEED and local authority structures and have sought to bring international figures and new ideas to Scotland. The issue of monitoring and evaluation of CPD has emerged both in the literature and in terms of advice offered to schools and Local Authorities. Some Authorities have offered substantial advice to schools on the place of CPD in the school improvement agenda and individual schools have, in turn, given advice to staff.

POINTS FOR REFLECTION

1 Can schools learn from good practice elsewhere? What conditions need to be present for such practice to 'transfer' successfully?

2 How can the impact of CPD on learning and teaching be evaluated?

3 What evaluation takes place in your establishment?

9 Better teachers – betters schools?

'Lots of people talk to animals,' said Pooh.
'Maybe, but...'
'Not very many *listen*, though,' he said.
'That's the problem,' he added.
Winnie the Pooh, A.A. Milne

Listening to teachers... and to teachers of teachers

Since the mid-1960s, there has been a worldwide quest to discover the key to school effectiveness. The early American studies (Coleman *et al.*, 1966; Jencks *et al.*, 1972) seemed to suggest that schools did not make a difference, at least not a significant difference. The so-called 'school effect' was calculated at around fifteen per cent. Thus, of all the influences on a young person's life chances, school contributed only around fifteen per cent. And, since the other 85 per cent – made up of a mixture of family background, social class, the peer group, ethnicity, and so on – was much more significant in its impact, the general conclusion was that schooling, by itself was unlikely to make a difference to young people's lives.

However, as discussed in Chapter 7, in 1979, Michael Rutter and his team challenged these assumptions in their seminal work, *Fifteen Thousand Hours*. Based on research in London secondary schools, they concluded that schools could in fact make a difference and that two schools serving similar catchment areas could have quite different outcomes as measured by examination results, attendance rates and patterns of behaviour. The key to a successful school was its *ethos*, a term which has since entered the vocabulary of education, and which they defined as 'the quality of relationships' in a school. Since this study was published, the school effectiveness movement has grown worldwide, with a multiplicity of studies, looking at a whole range of variables and often concluding with lists of characteristics of a 'good' school. In 1996, MacBeath *et al.* in *Schools Speak for Themselves*, listed the key characteristics of an effective school, derived from the most influential studies to date:

School climate	a safe place *Lightfoot 1983* good repair and maintenance *Rutter 1979* participation in extra-curricular activities *Coleman 1982*
Relationships	a sense of community *Purkey and Smith 1983* student-teacher rapport *Trisman 1976* positive teacher-pupil relations *Rutter 1979*
Classroom climate	orderly classrooms *Lipitz 1984* freedom from disruption *Hersch 1981* stimulating classroom environment *Walberg 1987* efficient organisation of class work *Mortimore 1988*
Support for teaching	strong staff development *Purkey and Smith 1983* teacher social interaction and dialogue *Little 1984* small classes in early years *Achilles 1993* teachers' internal locus of control *Evertson 1980*
Support for learning	the importance of praise *Brophy and Good 1986* homework given out and maked *Rutter 1979* prompt feedback on homework *Turner 1985* active role for teachers in helping pupils *Mortimore 1994*
Recognition of achievement	achievement orientation *Brookover 1979* success is celebrated *Lipitz 1982* positive reporting of achievement *Murphy 1982*
Time and resources	per pupil expenditure *Hedges 1994* time is protected *Murphy 1982*

Organisation and communication	effective communication *Lee, Bryk & Smith 1993* involvement of teachers in planning *Mortimore 1988* involvement of teachers in development planning *Mortimore 1988*
Equity	feeling of belonging *Behling 1982* school catering for all its pupils *Cuttance 1987* targeted praise and encouragement *Smith & Tomlinson 1989*
Home-school links	parental involvement in reading projects *Epstein 1987* the alterable curriculum of the home *Walberg 1984* initiating contact with parents and sending home good news *Squires 1983*

(1996: p.27)

The late 1980s and the early1990s had begun to see the emergence of the 'school improvement' school, which sought to look at the kinds of interventions which were associated with improvement in various aspects of school life. The focus was on how schools, with or without the support of 'critical friends', could improve by dint of their own actions. Often these studies looked at how systems, sometimes imposed by Government, such as School Development Planning, Performance Indicators; Audits of practice; Staff Development and Appraisal etc., were associated with school improvement.

The major feature of the school effectiveness studies was that they looked at inputs and outputs and they controlled for variables such as social class, gender, ethnicity, behaviour, and so on, and tried to find out why some schools apparently had better results than others. The school improvement studies tended to look at systems and processes and attempted to give advice to schools and to government about what schools should do to improve. The focus was often at the school level, with a heavy emphasis on management systems and leadership. Michael Fullan and Andy Hargreaves, together and separately became the most influential figures in this field, writing a series of highly readable books on school improvement using the title, *What's worth fighting for…?* looking in turn at the school, headship and education.

The missing link, however, was the teacher. Since the (in)famous Neville Bennet study, *Teaching Styles and Pupil Progress* (1976), it was as if the role of the teacher had become subsumed in the whole school system. The school effect was the key focus and the 'teacher effect' had, apparently got lost along the way. It was not that the researchers were unaware of the central role of the teacher, but that the studies were unable to focus sharply enough. Some important studies were produced (Delamont and Galton, 1986) which tried to make sense of what went on in the classrooms of effective teachers, but the policy focus continued to be on the school as an organisation. In the late 1990s, Professor Carol Fitzgibbon began to draw attention to the teacher effect and argued that it could as much as three times greater than the school effect (*TESS*, Sept 2004). Around the same time, Paul Black and Professor Dylan William were developing a set of ideas about teachers in classrooms which has become known as Assessment (is) for Learning. Their booklet, *Inside the Black Box* (2000), has become one of the most influential documents in recent educational history in the UK, and it draws on a large body of research evidence from around the world on the interventions which teachers make that are associated with improved pupil learning. They have crystallised these into four key elements:

- Sharing objectives of the learning with pupils.
- Teacher questioning.
- Constructive feedback.
- Self- and peer-assessment.

As a result of the publication of *Inside the Black Box*, and subsequent titles in the series, there are now national programmes across the UK, designed to engage teachers in discussions about how they can improve the learning of all of their pupils. At the heart of the programmes is CPD and it would appear that the pendulum is now beginning to swing from the managerialist approach to school improvement towards one which looks at what teachers do, individually and collectively, in classrooms to improve young people's life chances. Thus listening to teachers talk about what they do and why they do it;

what they think is successful and why they think so and how they adapt their classroom approaches, has become a key part of the improvement process. The concept of the reflective practitioner is now taking on a more prominent role now that CPD is at the heart of professional practice.

Better teachers, better schools – the contribution of CPD

The title of Goodlad's influential work (1994) can be expressed as a question or as a statement. What comes first, good teachers or good teacher education programmes? In the post-McCrone context, teacher education programmes must include more than simply Initial Teacher Education. It has to encompass, we have argued above, the probationary period, the Chartered Teacher Programme, the Scottish Qualification for Headship, the vast array of postgraduate leadership and management programmes and, of course, CPD in general. From ITE to retiral, teachers are now expected to be active players in their own professional development. But, what contribution can CPD make to this process?

Goodlad's thesis is that 'teacher education' is too important to be left to any one part of the system. He proposes 'centres of pedagogy' which would involve partnerships among universities (particularly the arts and sciences), school districts (encompassing, in the Scottish context, SEED and local authorities) and schools. These would be centres of enquiry into how humans learn and how they can best be taught. His main contention is that 'better teachers shape better schools' (1994: p. 271) and that 'even better teachers will encounter grave difficulties in fulfilling the educational mission of schools if other agencies, especially the home, fail in their nurturing, educative role.' (1994: p. 271). Goodlad argues for 'the community ecosystem of human service agencies' (1994: p. 271), not unlike that proposed the Scottish Executive's document *New Community Schools: a Prospectus* (1997). For Goodlad, the process of 'renewal' which must take place within teacher education must encompass what we in Scotland would call Continuing Professional Development.

Fullan and Hargreaves (1992) argue that:

A teaching force that is more skilled and flexible in its teaching strategies and more knowledgeable about its subject matter is a teaching force more able to improve the achievements of its pupils.

(1992: p. 2)

They suggest that while this is something of a truism, the difficulty has been that there has not always been a consensus on what constitutes 'good teaching'. They go on to argue that, 'teacher development…involves more than changing teachers' behaviour. It also involves changing the person the teacher is.' (1992: p. 7), and suggest that, 'the importance of the teacher as a person is receiving growing acceptance in the teacher development literature and among educational administrators.' (1992: p. 8).

While many teachers may be a little sceptical about the educational administrators aspect of Hargreaves and Fullan's claim, it is, nevertheless, true that a decade on, *A Teaching Profession for the 21st Century* seemed intent on putting the teacher at the centre of the school improvement agenda. Indeed, it could be said that the McCrone enquiry was acting on Hargreaves and Fullan's belief that: 'Critical reflection will not take place if there is neither time nor encouragement for it. Teachers will learn little from each other if they work in persistent isolation' (1992: p. 13).

For them, leadership is about creating the climate where teachers are supported to be reflective of their own and their colleagues' practice as part of their collaborative professional development. Indeed it is this collaborative culture that Hargreaves, in an individual contribution to the book, recommends as being the most fruitful conditions for improvement, provided, that is, the collegiality is not 'contrived'. Indeed, he draws out the distinctions between 'collaborative cultures' and 'contrived collegiality' (1992: p. 235), arguing that the latter is more 'masculine' in its characteristics. His conclusion is clear:

Attempts at teacher development and educational change will meet with little success unless they engage with the purposes of the teacher, unless they acknowledge the person the teacher is and unless they adjust to the slow pace of human growth that takes place in the individual and collective lives of the teachers.

(1992: p. 236)

CPD – one of the change forces?

Michael Fullan's *Change Forces* trilogy has mapped out a conceptual framework (see Chapter 7) for the understanding of organisational change. In the latest of the books, *Change Forces with a Vengeance* (2003), he argues, with echoes of Goodlad (above) that there is need for change at three levels – the school, the Local Authority (district) and the state if 'educational transformation' is to be achieved. Drawing on the work of Elmore (2002), Fullan argues that the system needs to invest in its teachers if it wants to build the 'capacities' needed to produce improvement in a school. Fullan's book is predicated on what he calls 'complexity theory' and quotes Ralph Stacey, (2001) 'The future of an organisation is perpetually constructed in the conversational exchanges of its members as they carry out their tasks.' (2003: p. 181).

Borrowing the terminology from Matthew Lipman's philosophical approach to thinking skills (1991), Fullan quotes Wenger, McDermott and Snyder in suggesting that organisations need to become 'communities of practice', 'groups of people who share a concern, a set of problems, or a passion about a topic, and who deepen their knowledge and expertise in this area by interacting on ongoing basis...' (2003: p. 4).

However, Fullan is adamant that such communities could become 'sterile', simply reinforcing the members' existing bad practice. He suggests that organisations which are led from the centre or which have 'heroic' leaders are less likely to be effective. The alternative is 'distributed leadership', where the organisation's knowledge is less in its databases than in its people, where people make decisions about the importance of knowledge held by the organisation and where the social systems are more important than the technical systems.

In this kind of organisation, knowledge sharing is the key. In the school setting, CPD is often the main vehicle for such sharing, where people have time to think, to discuss and to exchange insights into common problems. Fullan's complexity theory, when applied to the school setting, can be unsettling. A state of uncertainty, or, as Hoban (2002) describes it, 'intellectual unrest', may not be an attractive proposition for most teachers but, they argue, it is a necessary precursor of learning. They suggest that where discussions are characterised by all-out conflict or by complete avoidance, it is a sure sign that people are not prepared to listen to one another.

Performance management

For Fullan, 'Training' and 'Time' are key issues in any change process. One of the elements is performance management which 'at its best provides opportunity for dialogue, coaching, trying out, therefore building belief in professional judgement' (2003: p. 84). In the Scottish context, Reeves *et al.* (2002) argue that performance management and CPD should be part of the same framework. They trace the origin of performance management back to Jim Callaghan's 1976 Ruskin College speech which signalled a national concern about 'standards', through the New Right policies of Margaret Thatcher and Keith Joseph in the 1980s, and finally to New Labour's strategies to ensure compliance at the school level. In England and Wales, the power of the LEAs was reduced by devolving management control to school level. The concept of the self-managing school was born (Caldwell and Spinks, 1988) and central government produced a whole series of 'indicators' of progress as part of its approach to compliance. Schools were now being measured in terms of examination success and parental choice, through inspections and published reports, and via compulsory management processes such as school development planning.

Reeves *et al.* (2002) draw a distinction between an 'accountability' approach and a 'professional development' approach. They chart the troubled history of 'appraisal' in England and Wales and firmly locate performance management in the context of the New Labour Government's aim to modernise the profession. They see as the most positive aspect of the Government's strategy the commitment 'to establish, for the first time, the entitlement of teachers to high-quality professional development in response to their identified needs' (2002: p. 24). The dangers of performance-related pay (PRP) are not lost on the authors, and they point out that 'the output of teachers is the education of their teachers, which is multi-dimensional and not easy to measure' (2002: p. 24). Their view is that 'teaching is based on teamwork and co-operative effort' and as such any attempt through PRP to place teachers in competition with one another is misguided.

It is this aspect of performance management which is problematic in the Scottish context. The attempt by Michael Forsyth in the late 1980s to force Staff Development *and Appraisal* [my emphasis] on the teaching profession in Scotland was met with a mix of opposition (at the teaching union level) and refusal to implement (at the school level). The problem for Scottish teachers sprang from suspicion of Forsyth's motives and from the hierarchical, top-down, civil service-based model of SDA being proposed. There was little in the way of genuine consultation, and, as Reeves *et al.* point out, 'implementation was haphazard and largely unsuccessful' (2002: p. 25).

The DfEE, in 2001, outlined its rationale for high quality professional development:

> ...we know from talking to schools that a commitment to the development of every member of staff – teachers and support staff – frequently leads to the creation of an open, supportive and collaborative culture across the school; greater self-esteem, self-confidence and enthusiasm; better quality learning; better quality teaching; a real desire among staff to continue learning; and a greater capacity in the school as a whole for continuing self improvement.
>
> (In Reeves et al. 2002: p. 35)

It is interesting to note that the basis for these observations is cited as 'talking to schools'. This may be a conscious attempt to distance the DfEE from the research literature on the premise that schools are more impressed by what other schools say. But it does beg the question as to who is meant by 'schools'. Is it senior managers or is it all of the staff? Do classroom teachers feel that there is a genuine commitment on the part of government to 'the development of every member of staff'. Do they feel it is present within their senior managers? Reeves *et al.* argue that 'school-based professional development' will lead to 'the teachers and schools required of the twenty-first century' (2002: p. 38). Indeed, they argue that such a strategy will deliver higher teacher morale and motivation than is possible through any PRP scheme.

CPD – a role for universities?

In Scotland, Initial Teacher Education (ITE) is now the preserve of University Faculties of Education. Previously, it was the role of Colleges of Education (or, previously, Teacher Training Colleges) to carry out that function. Colleges always had a role in CPD (or in-service training), but now the question has to be posed against the backdrop of a new improvement agenda;

'What can universities contribute to the professional development of teachers?'

In 1996, the United States National Commission on Teaching and America's Future published a report entitled '*What Matters Most: Teaching for America's Future*'. The report proposes that several 'fatal distractions' need to be addressed, namely some of the myths surrounding teaching, including the assertion that anyone can teach, that teachers don't work hard enough and that teacher education is not of much use (Reiman and Thies-Sprinthall 1999).

There are also belief systems – some might question whether they are myths – around teacher educators. Howey (1995) has argued that American teacher educators 'are, frankly, limited in their pedagogical abilities.' The 'frankly' suggests that the writer is aware of the controversial nature of such a claim, but goes on to describe college classrooms as 'truly private sanctuaries'. These sentiments echo those of Clark (1992) who claimed that teacher educators had been silent on important policy debates, that colleges had often responded to teacher shortages by dropping key aspects of teacher training requirements and that many programmes in American universities were 'ineffective'.

In Scotland, these sentiments have rarely surfaced so explicitly, except when the New Right policies of the Thatcher Government were directed towards teacher education. There was a strong sense that Teacher Training Colleges, throughout the UK, were hotbeds of liberalism and progressive ideas, the very ideas associated in the minds of the New Right thinkers such as Sir Keith Joseph, and latterly, Chris Woodhead, HMSCI, with the 'failures' of the comprehensive system. From the perspective of public-school-educated Ministers, teacher training was not only unnecessary, it was part of the problem. Thus, ways of preparing people to be teachers which diminished the role of the Colleges and Faculties of Education, seemed attractive. Mentoring schemes, apprenticeship schemes, training schools have all been mooted in the past, and Initial Teacher Education was reviewed in 2004. However, in Scotland, the contribution of the universities to teacher development, while not entirely free of criticism, has been acknowledged as being important. The key initiatives of the Standard for Full Registration, Chartered Teacher and Scottish Qualification for Headship have all involved partnerships involving universities. Indeed, this partnership approach has been a distinctive feature of these developments in Scotland. However, there remains a school of thought which sees the school, or in Scotland, the Local Authority, as being the most appropriate locus for teacher professional development, at least the elements which are *post* ITE. Now that the recommendations of the *McCrone Report* on the probationary period have been implemented, ensuring at least one year's unbroken placement for teachers with a 0.3 element of the working week devoted to CPD, the ITE element can no longer be seen in isolation from the rest of CPD and, in this context, Local Authorities may wish to be more centrally involved in the *whole* process of teacher development.

In 2004, a new player entered this arena, namely the Hunter Foundation, a charitable organisation established by a successful Scottish entrepreneur with a commitment to promote not just enterprise education, but improvement in the system as a whole. Drawing on the Carnegie Corporation of New York's project, *Teachers for a New Era*, the Hunter Foundation used some its money to lever contributions from central government to fund a scheme to implement and evaluate a similar programme in Scotland. *Teachers for a New Era* has three broad design principles:

1 A teacher education programme should be guided by a respect for evidence;
2 Faculty in the disciplines of the arts and sciences must be fully engaged in the education of prospective teachers;
3 Education should be understood as an academically taught clinical practice profession.

The scope of this initiative is the pre-service and the induction (or probationary) period of teacher education. It is based on recent research in the United States which concludes that 'the quality of the teacher is the most important cause of pupil achievement.' Its genesis is the US report *A Nation at Risk* (1983) which pointed the way towards a fully integrated approach to teacher education.

Of the three design principles, the first seems the least problematic. A research-led, evidence-based approach seems the right way to go. The focus on pupil learning and its relationship to teaching approaches is what has characterised much of the recent debate around raising achievement and school improvement.

However, the other design principles are less straightforward. The focus on the arts and sciences, on one level, seems reasonable since a broad definition of both could encompass most subjects in the school curriculum. However, a closer reading of the rationale for this design principle reveals an assertion that while:

> a broad consensus exists that teachers preparing to teach at the secondary level ought to possess an academic major in the discipline they intend to teach…there is no similar consensus…on what should be the appropriate academic major for a candidate preparing to teach at the elementary level.'

The issue of the arts and sciences turns out to be one of academic specialism versus generalism, arising from a belief on the part of the sponsors of the programme that each discipline has a 'core structure' which has to be mastered if someone is to make the subject accessible to learners. It is further suggested that elementary teachers have only a 'synthetic' understanding of some of the disciplines they have to teach. This stance is at the very least debatable as a starting point. However, if the programme is true to its own principles, then the evidence base for such a view will, itself, need to be robust.

The third principle may be the most difficult of all to reconcile with traditional Scottish approach to teacher education. 'Teaching as an academically taught clinical practice profession' does not sit easily with the kind of language normally used in education discourse. The assertion that 'pedagogy lies at the heart of education' is not controversial until the phrase 'as an academic enterprise' is added. There are many educators who would argue that teaching is more than simply an *academic* endeavour. It is, however, the word 'clinical' which is not familiar in the Scottish context. *Teachers for a New Era* is predicated on the assumption that 'Excellent teaching is a clinical skill.' Pupils are 'clients', classrooms are 'clinics' and the probationary period is 'residency'. However, this terminology masks a philosophy which may not be too far removed from that which characterises the Scottish approach. Leaving aside the claim, discussed above, that 'there is a knowledge base for teaching that is taught and learned in academic settings', the emphasis on education being 'developmental' and the suggestion that the 'clinicians [should] not act upon the client, but…assist the client's growth and development' sits well with the Scottish child-centred approach. The Carnegie Corporation sets out five key areas of clinical practice to be developed:

Pedagogy

Teachers will be expected to develop a curriculum which engages pupils, which builds on prior learning and promotes deep understanding. Links with the family are encouraged as are collaborative work with colleagues. Formative assessment, a range of teaching strategies and recognition of learning styles are all suggested as key aspects of pedagogy.

Schools as clinics

This issue may be more controversial. The proposal is that a number of schools are designated as 'practicing [sic] schools' where senior management and staff will have an enhanced role, in collaboration with University staff, in supervising and assessing student teachers. The essential element here is that teachers will assess pupil learning as a function of the success of students' teaching.

Teachers on faculty appointment

This is akin to Associate Lecturerships already in place in some universities but with more status. 'Outstanding experienced teachers' would be selected and given an appointment at a senior level (in America it might be professor of practice or adjunct professor) with a formal role in the preparation of future teachers.

Residency

The idea is that this will be a two-year period with mentoring and supervision. As has been discussed earlier, the McCrone Report has introduced a one-year probationary period in Scotland, with an enhanced CPD element. It is not clear from the documentation whether the length of time is the key issue here or the quality and extent of the support. However, it is clear that the *Teachers for a New Era* proposal on residency goes beyond the current Scottish provision.

Preparation of candidates for professional growth

The concept of 'communities of colleagues' is introduced, both within subjects on an area basis and across subjects in the school context. CPD or 'professional renewal' (cf. Goodlad, 1994) would be the key to professional growth.

Teachers for a New Era represents both an opportunity and a threat to our established ways of doing things in the context of Initial Teacher Education. The American terminology and some of the assumptions which underpin the concept of 'clinical practice' may make it threatening but the account of the pedagogy associated with effective pupil learning would be familiar to Scottish teachers, particularly those involved with initiatives such as thinking skills or Assessment is for Learning. In the context of the review of Initial Teacher Education, it will be interesting to note the outcome of the Scottish development of this American programme.

SUMMARY

Since the mid-1960s, researchers worldwide have tried to identify the characteristics of effective schools, and since the 1990s have begun to focus on how schools improve their practice. With very few exceptions, the emphasis was on the school-level factors, and as a consequence of some of the research findings, managerial solutions were offered by policy-makers and, in some respects, 'efficiency' was confused with 'effectiveness'. More recently, a number of studies have demonstrated that the 'teacher effect' can be greater than the school effect in terms of its impact on young people's levels of achievement. Initiatives in the US and in Europe have sought to put Initial Teacher Education and CPD at the heart of the improvement agenda. The emphasis has been on the collaborative nature of CPD, in the belief that real collaboration, accompanied by trust and an altruistic professionalism, will enhance the effectiveness and impact on student learning of CPD. The role of the Universities in ITE and CPD has been the subject of debate in the US for the last twenty years and is emerging here too. A link between the two is the *Teachers for the New Era* initiative funded by the Hunter Foundation in Scotland.

POINTS FOR REFLECTION

1 How useful has the literature in schools effectiveness and school improvement been to your professional development? Has any one book, or study or writer influenced your thinking? In what ways?

2 Do you agree that the main focus should be on the teacher in the classroom? If so, how can such a focus help schools to improve their practice overall?

3 What role do you see for universities in ITE and/or CPD?

10 CPD – a brave new world?

> Here is Edward Bear coming down stairs,
> bump, bump, bump on the back of his head
> behind Christopher Robin. It is, as far as he
> knows, the only way of coming down stairs,
> but sometimes he thinks there really must be a
> better way, if only he could stop bumping
> for a moment and think of it.
>
> *Winnie the Pooh*, A. A. Milne

'Megatrends' in education

When Michael Fullan coined the phrase 'problems are our friends', he most probably did not do so gloomily. Indeed, his intention was the opposite. Problems are challenges which inspire us to reach new heights but more importantly from Fullan's point of view, they are more easily solved collaboratively than individually. Fullan's evaluation of the Numeracy and Literacy Hours in England pointed out that the gains that are likely to be made through the work of individual teachers in classroom delivering centrally produced programmes are likely to be short term and the effects are likely to level off in due course. If long-term, sustained and incremental improvements are being sought, then teachers need to be treated with some trust and they need to work together. CPD is one of the most important means whereby this collaboration can be fostered.

In her book, *Continuing Professional Development* (2000), Anna Craft cites Naisbitt and Aburdene who identify ten 'megatrends in education', and suggests that these might be 'a reference point with which to evaluate some of the changes in CPD which are currently in progress':

1 Formulating goals, deciding on goals and priorities and creating accountability frameworks will increasingly become the role of *central authorities*.

2 These will be informed by *national and global considerations*, especially in respect to curriculum. The education system will need, increasingly, to be responsive to national needs within a global economy.

3 State-funded schools will become *largely self-managing* within a national framework of accountability. Distinctions between these and privately funded schools will narrow.

4 *Concern* for the provision of a *quality* education for each individual will reach unprecedented levels.

5 Telecommunications and computer technology will contribute to the *dispersion of the educative function*. Much learning which currently occurs in schools or institutions at post-compulsory levels will occur at home and in the workplace.

6 The *basics in education will be reformulated and expanded* to include problem-solving, creativity and a capacity for lifelong learning and re-learning.

7 *The arts and spirituality*, defined broadly in each instance, will have a significantly expanded role to play in educating; there will be a high level of 'connectedness' in the curriculum.

8 *There will be many more women leaders* in education, including the most senior levels.

9 The *parent and community role* in education will be claimed or reclaimed.

10 *Those who support the work of schools (whether voluntarily or as part of their job) will be subject to deep concern for the quality of service.*

(Naisbit and Aburdene 1990: p. xvii)

Think global, act local – implications of megatrends for Scotland

1 Formulating goals, deciding on goals and priorities and creating accountability frameworks will increasingly become the role of *central authorities*.

In Scotland, these megatrends are already being played out. SEED and Local Authorities set goals and priorities, establish accountability frameworks through inspection, self-evaluation manuals and 'challenge and support teams' (CAST) and schools have to work within these.

Implications for CPD: the danger here is that professionals in schools feel disempowered and de-skilled if the locus of decision-making is outwith the school. Accountability can be a straitjacket or it can be liberating if trust is its starting point. Therefore, at a school and cluster level, CPD is needed to enable professionals to understand the goals and priorities and to develop self-evaluation processes which enable them to reflect on their own practices.

2 These will be informed by *national and global considerations*, especially in respect to curriculum. The education system will need, increasingly, to be responsive to national needs within a global economy.

The Ministerial Review Group on the Curriculum 3–18 has looked at developments in Tasmania, Norway, Finland and Singapore, amongst others. It has acknowledged that Scotland is not unique among developed countries in reviewing its curriculum.

Implications for CPD: there is a need to give some time for those people working within establishments to look at the 'big picture'. There should be some consideration of aims on a regular basis – aims of education, of the school and within the classroom. These discussions should involve as many of the stakeholders as possible, including the learners and should be in the context of global changes and education's contribution to them.

3 State-funded schools will become *largely self-managing* within a national framework of accountability. Distinctions between these and privately funded schools will narrow.

Delegation of management to schools began in the early 1990s in Scotland, pioneered by some of the Local Authorities and supported by the Scottish Office Education and Industry Department. However, Scotland did not take the same policy direction as England and schools did not opt out of Local Authority control to become fully self-managing. Indeed, some would argue that it is the continuing existence of strategic Local Authorities in Scotland which has contributed to its success in educational terms. As a consequence, there has been less convergence between the independent and state sectors in Scotland.

Implications for CPD: CPD remains a priority of each of the Local Authorities in Scotland working in partnership with the new national co-ordinator. While the Authorities themselves are no longer the principal *providers*, they tend to organise programmes of in-service courses delivered by a mix of local school-based staff or seconded development officers, university staff from Faculties of Education or private, commercial providers. In addition, national initiatives, such as Assessment is for Learning, fund and sponsor CPD opportunities. This national element increasingly included the independent schools sector, while some Authorities offer places to independent school staff on a full-cost basis.

4 *Concern* for the provision of a *quality* education for each individual will reach unprecedented levels.

The 'individualisation' or 'personalisation' of education is high on the political agenda in Scotland. Edinburgh Council espoused it as the cornerstone of its education policy in 2004, and the concept is widely referred to by New Labour politicians in London and in Edinburgh. Personal Learning Plans have become an embodiment of this policy and ICT is regarded as one of the ways in which it might, ultimately, be achieved. 'Quality' has been a central issue since the 1990s when Quality Assurance became the focus not just of central government but of Local Authorities (such as Strathclyde, which had Scotland's only local inspectorate, called the Quality Assurance Unit), and there have been productions of 'quality indicators' to guide managers within the system. It is this concern for quality which has fuelled the debate about 'Inclusion', with proponents seeing it as the vehicle for individualisation, while critics see the rights of the majority being compromised by a focus on the few.

Implications for CPD: CPD for teachers on Personal Learning Plans has initially targeted schools and staff working with young people with additional support needs. If Inclusion is to be successful as a national strategy, then CPD will need to be available for *all* staff who work with young people in schools, not just teachers and not just teachers who teach young people with additional support needs. Individualisation, or personalisation of education means meeting the needs of each young person and it implies valuing all of them equally. As Reueven Feuerstein has argued in his theory of *Structural*

Cognitive Modifiability, every human being can be a successful learner and if there are gaps in their basic prerequisites for successful learning these need to be addressed on an individual basis so that the individual can fulfil her/his potential as a learner and as a social being. However, Feuerstein also argues that 'geographical inclusion' is not enough. Simply placing a young person in a mainstream school is not inclusion if there is inadequate preparation of the young person, of the parents or carers and of the receiving teachers. This calls for a new and more radical strategic approach to CPD.

5 Telecommunications and computer technology will contribute to the *dispersion of the educative function*. Much learning which currently occurs in schools or institutions at post-compulsory levels will occur at home and in the workplace.

This has been a powerful vision since long before computers became universally accessible. Isaac Asimov, in his short story, *The Fun They Had*, describes a future where there are no schools and where children are educated at home, by robots. Work is geared uniquely to the needs of the individual and feedback from the robot is instantaneous. But the two children, a brother and sister, at the centre of the story, during one of their breaks, find a real book. On reading it, they learn of what schools were like in the twentieth century, with hundreds of young people of similar ages learning together. The story ends with the entrance once more of the robot and the inattention of the learners as they dream, wistfully, of the twentieth century children, and the fun they had.

So are we really any closer to a pattern of learning in which young people do not go to a building called a school from 9 a.m. to 3.30 p.m. five days a week, 38 weeks of the year? Distance Learning takes place in adult contexts and eLearning is beginning to make an impact there too. But there are no examples yet, in Scotland, of such models being applied to school-age learners. Crucially, it is not just the socialisation aspects of education which make schools important but their role in the acculturation of young people. Universal schooling was hard fought for and was really only achieved as recently as the end of the Second World War when secondary schooling became compulsory in Scotland. (My own parents never attended secondary schools in the 1930s, but instead finished their education around the age of thirteen in the Advanced Division of the primary school.)

The growth of the internet might make home learning more possible in the foreseeable future. The idea of the school as a 'hub' to which students go for certain activities which require social interaction and the intervention of teachers, surrounded by satellites, including the home, youth centres, cyber cafes, the workplace, and so on, seem more feasible now. It may be that learning becomes a life-long process and not squeezed into 15000 hours (Rutter, 1979) between the ages of three and eighteen. Of course it raises all sorts of practical issues such as accessibility of the internet, supervision of students' work, the role of parents and others in the learning process and the organisation of such a flexible system. The idea of a core curriculum with options could fit into such a system, and it could deliver the individualisation desired by the present Government. But it would be a change more radical than any other since the Industrial Revolution enabled society to see children as something other than wage earners.

Implications for CPD: teachers need to become comfortable with ICT. NOF training, as Conlon has argued, failed in many cases to give teachers the confidence and skills they needed. Now, SEED-funded 'Materclasses' are being rolled out across Scotland and the early indications are that these are being well received. However, there is still an concern that ICT has failed to make the impact expected of it in terms of improving learning and teaching not because of problems with hardware or lack of software, but because we lack a pedagogy which comfortably accommodates ICT. Is it a tool for learning? What is the teacher's role in mediating the learning? Does it facilitate co-operative as well as individualised learning? Is it adaptable to different learning styles? All these and other questions need to be addressed, ideally in a CPD context, before teachers will be able to make the best use of ICT in the classroom.

6 *The basics in education will be reformulated and expanded* to include problem-solving, creativity and a capacity for lifelong learning and re-learning.

There is a growing body of literature which argues that a system of schooling designed for a stable and relatively unchanging world will not suffice in the twenty-first century. David Perkins has argued that we need to educate young people for the 'unknown' and not simply for the known. Edward de Bono has suggested that creativity is the key to a successful society in the twenty-first century, and an education system built on the classical pillars of rationality and truth, will not suffice. Michael Fullan has also made the case for looking at schooling in the context of complexity theory and has argued that current structures will not serve the needs of pupils or teachers well in the twenty-first century.

The 'basics' in education have long been a political battleground. John Major's famous cry of 'back to basics' in the early 1990s was about social and moral values as well as educational objectives. His Senior Chief Inspector of Schools, was, and remains, a fierce opponent of anything in schooling which does *not* focus on the basics. He has been scathing of liberal, progressive methods in education, and has singled out Thinking Skills as a villain of the piece arguing that there is no place for it until all children have 'mastered the basics'.

The three Rs – reading, (w)riting and reckoning – have been considered to be the basics since schooling began. Can 'problem-solving, creativity and a capacity for lifelong learning and re-learning' really be considered in the same way? The key to this conundrum lies, perhaps, in not seeing these two interpretations of 'the basics' as mutually exclusive. If the twenty-first century does see technological and social change of an even greater magnitude than the twentieth, it is clear that the traditional patterns of learning will not suffice. If, as it has been suggested, around twenty per cent of the jobs which children currently in P1 will end up doing, do not currently exist, then it is also likely that fewer people will do the same job for life. Change is likely to be the only constant, and so people will need to be prepared for learning new skills throughout their (working) lives. Thus one of the basics will be, as John Nisbet (1986) has long argued, learning how to learn (metacognition). Problem-solving and creativity will be fundamental since new problems will need new solutions.

However, the 'basics' of reading and writing and numeracy will not disappear. The Internet has not lessened the need for literacy, it has simply changed the parameters. Computers can do calculations much faster than humans, but people will still need to understand 'the nature and purpose of mathematics' (5–14 Mathematics). In other words, the basics have been expanded and the challenge for the education system is to prepare teachers to meet this challenge and to develop a curriculum which enables it to happen.

Implications for CPD: at any one time in Scottish education there is a plethora of initiatives, emanating from the Scottish Executive or from individual Local Authorities, aimed at improving learning and teaching and raising standards of achievement. In recent years, Assessment is for Learning; Better Behaviour, Better Learning; Thinking Skills; Creativity in Education; Enterprise; Citizenship; The Health Promoting School; Co-operative Learning; The Critical Skills Programme, to name but a few, have been promoted by central or local government. These initiatives represent a potentially bewildering array of advice to schools and teachers, the impression is given that each initiative has to be done separately.

One potential role for CPD is to allow teachers to make sense of these initiatives, looking at their key features and identifying a range of strategies which are common to all of them. In this way, all teachers can contribute some aspects of all these initiatives, while others, perhaps specialists, can deliver other elements. In this way, teachers can 'join up' the initiatives and create a classroom climate where assessment *is* for learning, where pupils behave better because they are learning more successfully, where creativity and enterprising attitudes are promoted and pupils are encouraged to work collaboratively in a self-directed manner. As the pupils understand more about why they are learning and what strategies they have available, then they learn to make informed choices and become able to learn how to learn.

7 *The arts and spirituality*, defined broadly in each instance, will have a significantly expanded role to play in educating; there will be a high level of 'connectedness' in the curriculum.

The place of the arts and spirituality in the curriculum in Scotland continues to be a matter of debate. The Scottish Executive launched its arts and culture strategy in 2000 but its impact on the education system has been slight. At present, the arts are represented in the curriculum by Expressive Arts in the 5–14 programme and by Creative and Aesthetic subjects in middle and later secondary school. In the 5–14 programme, fifteen per cent of the curriculum is allocated to Expressive Arts while in the secondary the percentage may vary a little but for most pupils it will not be more than fifteen per cent, and possibly less. It would be acknowledged by most educationists that whatever term is used to describe the arts, the reality is that they are still seen as *minority* subjects within the curriculum. However, it is worth noting that this is not so everywhere. In 2004, the Reggio Emiglia region of Italy celebrated 40 years of a curriculum which in the early years of children's education places a huge emphasis on the arts and on creativity. Even here in Scotland, while time allocations seem niggardly in comparison to Reggio's, when the Rationale section of each of the 5–14 documents are examined, it is Expressive Arts which places most emphasis on thinking skills, on creativity and personal growth.

Implications for CPD: any increase in the amount of time given to Expressive Arts in the early years and primary curriculum will have implications for CPD. Many teachers worry about their level of expertise in music, art, drama and the rest and will require increased levels of CPD. The use of specialist staff, from primary and secondary schools, and talented individuals from the wider community, might help, but teachers will want to feel more confident of their ability to promote the Expressive Arts, albeit with very young pupils.

The issue of interconnectedness may well be more difficult to achieve. It is, along with 'transfer', the Holy Grail of education. It involves teachers working together across sectors and across subject areas; it involves greater consistency in terms of pedagogy; and it involves more coherence in the way in which the curriculum is planned. All of these have implications for CPD, not just in its content but in the opportunities for teachers to work with colleagues, from within their own schools and from other schools. Thus, for example, instead of schools having in-service days individually, there should be more whole-cluster days when all the staff from the secondary and associated primaries, pre-5 and Additional Support Needs schools come together to share insights into aspects of learning and teaching. At the very least, it should happen on an annual basis.

8 There will be many more women leaders in education, including the most senior levels.

This phenomenon has already begun to happen, but the rate of progress is slow. In the secondary sector, where traditionally, men have dominated senior management posts, the situation across Scotland is patchy. In one, albeit small, local authority 50 per cent of the secondary headteachers are women. In another, larger, authority, there are no female secondary headteachers.

Nationally, the figure is around ten per cent. The percentage of Depute headteachers (post-McCrone) is higher than that for heads, but there is still a marked imbalance. In the early 1990s, Bill Gatherer and Paquita McMichael of Moray House College of Education, carried out some research into the perceptions of male and female depute headteachers and found that the latter were much less likely than their male counterparts to be looking forward to their next promotion (to headship) but, instead, were concerned about whether they were doing a good job at present and had, typically, less confidence in their ability to move to the next level of promotion. However, if current trends in teacher recruitment continue, it may be that the gender imbalance at senior staff level will resolve itself, simply because fewer men appear to be entering teaching in every sector.

Implications for CPD: it could be argued that, whatever your standpoint on this issue, it has few, if any, implications for CPD. However, it is possible to argue that the models of CPD may well change, reflecting a more collaborative, exploratory approach. The stand-up, expert-led presentations followed by an activity and feedback, may not suffice. Indeed, the very layout of such sessions, often with chairs laid out theatre-style and a screen and flip-chart out front, may seem inappropriate. It is much more likely that tables will be laid out cabaret-style, with leaderless groups engaged in exploratory and creative tasks, probably preceded by some Brain Gym. The power relationships between facilitator and participants may well change and the principles of androgogy will be observed. 'Ah tel ye/Ah telt ye' has been as applicable to the CPD arena as it has to the classroom in Scotland.

9 The *parent and community role* in education will be claimed or reclaimed.

New Community Schools or Integrated Community Schools as they have become known, are the Scottish embodiment of parental and community partnerships, at least in theory. The role of parents in education became politicised in the 1980s and 1990s when the Thatcher Government introduced a series of measures dubbed 'parent power'. Parental choice was elevated to central plank of education policy, with choice of school, introduction of School Boards (with a view to allowing schools to 'opt out' of Local Authority control) and even a proposal to introduce vouchers for pre-school places, all introduced or promoted by the UK Government for Scotland. In response to this onslaught, Strathclyde Regional Council appointed a Development Officer (Parents) who worked with parental organisations to give them a voice in shaping education policy. His development of Parent Prompts, a set of parent-friendly resources to support family learning in the home based on the 5–14 Strands, attracted international attention. Since then, the new unitary authorities have sought to work with parents' organisations from pre-5 through to post-16. The Scottish Parent Teacher Council has become an influential body and its main spokesperson, Judith Gillespie, has often been invited to participate in policy-making at a national level. At a local level, schools have sought new ways to engage with parents, with differing degrees of success, the best practice often being found at the pre-school level.

The relationship between schools and their communities has often been a troubled one. No one, it seems, wants to live beside a school, especially a secondary school. Pupils are often stereotyped as unruly, impolite and noisy and local shopkeepers, pedestrians and users of public transport often see these pupils, often in crowds, as part of the problem. Even the school building has not always been open to community use. In the 1980s, Strathclyde Region pioneered 'joint use' of schools' sports facilities, often building new entrances and new sports areas, to be used by the school during the day and the community at night and at weekends. The Community School in Lothian Region was an attempt to make the whole school a part of the community, with teaching and other staff appointed on 'sessional' contracts to enable them to work in the evenings and at weekends. Some schools in the former Renfrew Division of Strathclyde, were built with Community Wings, and had a Depute Headteacher (Community) to co-ordinate activities and access. None of these were unalloyed successes, and Integrated Community Schools are the latest attempts to bring the schools and their communities closer together.

Implications for CPD: Working with parents to empower them to support their children's learning is now the focus of much of the CPD in schools across the country. Initiatives such as the Home School Employment Partnership (Boyd and Bowes, 1996) were well funded and short term. Now, in Councils across

Scotland there is a plethora of initiatives, from Family Learning to Thinking Skills, geared towards involving parents in their children's learning. Historically, pre-5 establishments and primary schools have run parents' workshops on areas of the curriculum. Now the focus has shifted to giving parents the skills and confidence to learn with their children, indeed to offer SPICE – support, praise, interest, challenge and encouragement – to their offspring. When Strathclyde introduced Supported Study (now Study Support) in 1991, it encouraged schools to use adults from the community as well as teachers and to offer them CPD where needed. MacBeath *et al.* (1996) found one school in Wales which used retired people from the community, with training, to support children's reading on a one-to-one basis.

10 *Those who support the work of schools (whether voluntarily or as part of their job) will be subject to deep concern for the quality of service.*

The issue of quality is one which has dominated the educational debate since the 1980s. With concepts often borrowed from the world of industry and commerce, 'total quality management' gave way to the 'quality process' and now to the quest for 'continuing improvement'. Local Authorities under a Conservative Government were under pressure to put services out to compulsory competitive tender. Under a Labour government, best value reviews must be carried out on a regular basis to demonstrate that Council Tax payers are getting value for money.

Within education, the language of 'audit', 'school development planning' and 'performance management' entered the realms of the school and HMI developed 'performance indicators' to be used for school self-evaluation and for the inspection process. In recent years, these, too, have become 'quality pointers'. The publication of inspection reports, the creation of league tables of schools by examination performance and the requirement for schools and local authorities to produce standards and quality reports on a regular basis, all confirm the dominance of the 'quality agenda'.

Implications for CPD: In the 1990s there was a veritable explosion of management courses, often with a direct link to school self-evaluation. The more sophisticated schools became at this, the less external inspection would be needed, wouldn't it?

Well, actually, the frequency of inspections has increased since the early 1990s. There seems to be a paradox at work here. What is needed, surely, is an increase in the kind of CPD which empowers schools, and clusters of schools, with the support of their authority staff, to be truly self-evaluative. HMIE could then operate a 'light touch' inspection process, focusing on identifying good practice where it exists and finding mechanisms, including national CPD opportunities, to disseminate the practice. CPD, of the kind promoted by Fullan and others, would address the quality agenda by bringing together all of the stakeholders and enabling them to make genuine contributions.

The draft report of the Ministerial Review Group on the Curriculum 3–18, argues that everyone in society has a stake in the outcomes of schooling. This can manifest itself in a concern for quality generally or an interest in improving learning and teaching specifically, but the effect is the same. The curriculum is not an ideological battleground contested by vested interests, but a manifestation of what a society hold to be important if its aspirations are to be realised. CPD is part of the way in which professionals can interact with others and one of the best ways of achieving recognition of the work which schools do to enable all young people to realise their potential.

A way ahead for CPD in Scotland?

There is evidence in the short time since the McCrone Report that CPD has emerged as the vehicle for change and improvement in Scottish education. This series of books is, in itself, testimony to the realisation that reading, reflection, research and collaborative working are at the heart of teachers' professionalism and a vehicle for them to enhance their partnership roles with others who are engaged in the education of young people. The Review of the Curriculum 3–18 may turn out to be an important event in Scottish education, with far-reaching implications for how the curriculum is conceptualised, implemented and tailored to meet the changing demands of the twenty-first century. What is certain is that no significant improvement in the education of young people will result unless CPD is the vehicle for sustainable change to take place.

The concept of 'communities of innovation' or 'communities of practice' has emerged from the thinking of the Future

Learning and Teaching (FLaT) Reference Group and attention is turning to the mechanisms by which people in the world of education can work more collaboratively and create the capacity for improvement. Lessons from business and commerce as well as education are being learned and new technology is being explored as a means of bringing people and ideas together. At the local level – the individual establishment, the learning community, the council – high quality CPD which empowers people to work together in new ways is likely to emerge as the vital ingredient in the improvement process.

SUMMARY

A number of 'megatrends' in education have been identified and each of these has been looked at against a Scottish backdrop. From the globalisation of education to the impact of ICT; from the growing influence of women at all levels to the emphasis on quality; from the importance of spirituality to the enhanced role of parents and communities – all have a resonance in Scotland and have implications for CPD.

POINTS FOR REFLECTION

1 Which of the 'megatrends' do you find most challenging? How do you see it impacting on your part of the education service?

2 Can CPD deliver educational improvement? Discuss.

Appendix

An Introdution to Continuing Professional Development

1 **What is CPD?**
   Continuing Professional Development is an opportunity for teachers to enhance their professional competence. Activities are recorded in two ways, activities that take place within the 35-hour working week and an additional 35 hours per year that are outwith the working week. CPD has two components: CPD carried out within the working week, for example, in-service and the additional 35 hours per year.

2 **Are the additional 35 hours of CPD per year compulsory?**
   Yes, full implementation in August 2003 when 35 hours per year will be spent on CPD activities outwith the working week of 35 hours.

3 **When will it be introduced?**
   Phasing in begins from now with full implementation during session 2003/2004.

4 **Do in-service course activities and courses all count towards CPD?**
   Attendance at all courses/participation in all activities will be recorded by each individual teacher in their CPD Plan/Record. However, it is only the ones that take place outwith the school day that count towards the annual commitment of 35 hours.

5 **How will activities be recorded?**
   Each teacher will have a CPD Plan/Record. CPD folios will be required for the Chartered Teacher Grade.

6 **Will records be stored centrally?**
   Each member of staff will be responsible for the storage of records and keeping them up to date. They will be especially important as a part of Staff Development & Review interviews.

7 **Will staff be given guidance on completing CPD Records?**
   Yes, exemplars are included in the Council Guidelines on CPD (pages 17/18). Three samples from within school are also available.

8 **How will these records be monitored and by whom?**
   At certain times they will be monitored by line managers and the Staff Development Co-ordinator who will be required to make returns to the Council.

9 **Will NOF (Learning Schools Programme) training count towards the additional 35 hours of CPD?**
   Yes, provided activities are completed in your own time.

10 **Does this replace the existing Staff Development & Review process?**
   Yes. The CPD Plan/Record will be part of the revised Staff Development and Review process. (New SD&R Guidelines awaited.)

Opportunities for Staff Development

- Involvement in Staff Development and Review process
  Awareness of SL guidelines/decision to take up entitlement
  Reflection on professional practice
  Discussion of continuing development
  Agreed development areas on which to focus
  Identification/provision of support required

- Involvement as member of
  Curriculum Groups of Principal Teachers
  Working Parties/Steering Groups in county
  School Consultative Groups as representative
  School Task Groups
  Department Team Meeting

- Involvement in Shadowing/Working Alongside Colleagues
  Gaining experience of:
    Other curriculum areas
    Other teaching styles/approaches
    Particular aspects of education
    Particular role responsibilities

- Involvement with student placements
  In department/class
  Contributing to organised programme of inputs

- Involvement with In-School Probationer Programme
  As probationer
  As a teacher willing to offer support to probationers
  As Departmental colleague/Mentor
  As Principal Teacher
  As promoted Member of Staff with responsibility for
  Probationers
  As member of Probationer Support Group
  As contributor to Probationer Support Meetings/Inset
  sessions

- Involvement in Probationer Programme
  Attending probationer forum meetings/conferences
  Feeding back to school group after attendance at meeting/
  conferences

- **Involvement in Reflection/Evaluation of Practice**
  Classroom organisation and management
  Course/lesson planning
  New resources available
  Teaching and learning approaches
  Assessment strategies
  Staff supporting each other in self-evaluation through
    informal discussions about teaching
    more formalised classroom visits

- **Involvement with Support for Pupils Learning**
  Discussions with SfL/Speech and Language/Guidance
  Individual consideration of support needed
  Department discussion of support needed
  Compilation of bid for support for pupils/staff
  Working alongside support staff
    in co-operative teaching situations
    on development of materials

- **Involvement in Pupil Shadowing**

- **Involvement in Primary-Secondary Liaison Activities**
  As co-opted member of 5–14 Implementation Group for
  particular purpose/period of time
  As member of subject department:
    discussing curricular progression P7/S1
    linking with associated primaries
    attending meetings of Primary 7 teachers
    attending a meeting of Cluster Primary Heads
    leading inset/sharing experience with primary staff
    jointly producing pupil materials etc.

- **Involvement in formulation of School Policies**
  As member of the school group producing new school policy
  As member of the school group reviewing/amending existing
  policy
  Discussion of issues – departmental/cross curricular groups
  As an individual offering views as part of the consultation
  process
  As department team offering views as part of the
  consultation process

- **Involvement in Development Planning Activities**
  Reviewing current development plan targets
  Discussing/agreeing areas for departmental developments

Prioritising targets for inclusion in department development plan
Checking department plan against whole school plan
Monitoring of development plans by SMT link

- **Involvement in Department consideration of Advisory Services Catalogue**
  Awareness of the whole range of available subject courses
  Identification of courses targeted to particular areas
  Matching courses to School/Department development Plan targets
  Prioritising courses requested for coming session(s)

- **Involvement in In-service Provision – outwith school**
  Attendance at courses/Conferences/Quality Management Seminars
  Completion of Accredited Courses
  Sharing ideas with colleagues
  Evaluation of inputs/workshops
  Completing evaluation forms for Advisory Service
    immediately after in-service to assess course
    after period of time to assess impact
  Showing/discussing own copy to Staff Development Co-ordinator
  Feedback of information to own department/SMT
  Feedback to Task Group/Whole School
  Written report produced on issues covers

- **Involvement in In-Service Provision – within school**
  Identification of areas for school focus
  Participation in Inset Day Programmes
  Evaluation of Inset Day Programmes
  Contribution to Inset Day programmes – sharing experience/ideas as speaker/participant/group member, chair, reporter

- **Involvement in developing personal awareness**
  Through reading
    Times Educational Supplement Scotland
    Educational Books/Journals/Articles
    Newsletters/Information Updates:
      In-school   Weekly Bulletin
                       Learning/Behaviour Support
                       Group Work/Joint Assess. Team
                       Newsletter

External   Higher Still Development Updates
                  Learning & Teaching Matters
                  NGfL/SQA/SCRE/BJSE/BJLS/NASEN
                  etc.

- **Involvement in working with External Agencies**
  Psychological Services/Social Work/Universal Connection/
  Careers Service/Local Employers/Child and Family Service/
  School Nurse & Doctor/Speech Therapy/Occupational
  Therapy/Further Education/Higher Education, etc.

- **Involvement in activities to develop ICT Skills**
  Participation in   NOF Training – Learning School
                       Programme
                       Support sessions from our Teacher
                       Advisers
                       School In-service opportunities
                       In-service Council
  Incorporating ICT into classroom practice

- **Involvement in Piloting New Materials/Approaches/
  Initiatives**

Continuing Professional Development Plan/Record   (Draft Exemplar)

CPD Activity (Brief Description)	Planned CPD Activity Date(s) and Source				
	SDP	SD and R	Collective Time Activities	Devt. Day Prog	Other
Private Reading: Intro Maths for Physical Sciences					Aug-Dec
PG Cert in learning and Teaching: Learning Strategies Unit (Twilight)		April 2002			
In-service course on ICT in science	Sept 2001			Oct 2001	
In-service course on introduction to PASCO interface	Oct 2001			Dec 2001	
Development work: Physics int 2 assessment material	By Dec 2001				
Presentation on Classroom Visits				4 Mar 2002	
Standards and Quality; Self-evaluation and production of evaluative statements (Department meetings)	Sept March				
Preparation for SDandR/ SDand R discussion		Jan 2002			
Curriculum Dev; Materials for Advance Higher Physics Investigation Unit	By May 2002				
Attend Institute of Physics Annual		Feb 2002			
Child Protection workshop			Sept 2001		
New guidelines on environmental studies (Private reading)	Aug 2001				

Completion Date(s)	Time to Complete (Hours)		Comments/Evaluations	Date(s) of Review of CPD Plan/Record (SD and R Discussions
	Within 35 hr week	Outwith 35 hr week		
Dec 2001		2 hours	Updated knowledge of maths required to teach advanced higher physics	Jan 2002
		12 hours	Update skills – progressing well but very demanding of time	Jan 2002
	6 hours	2 hours	See evaluation sheet	Jan 2002
Dec 2001	3 hours	5 hours	See evaluation sheet Course tutor was excellent. This has benefitted whole department	Jan 2002
Jan 2002	3 hours	5 hours	Gained valuable experience in producing assessment items – good department exercise	Jan 2002
	1 hour		Think this could be worthwhile. I've read the guidelines	Jan 2002
By May 2002	Est 5 hours		Already had 2 meetings. Writing evaluative statements is more difficult than I thought it would be	Jan 2002
Jan 2002	1 hour	2 hours	Reflection time is good	Jan 2002
	Est 4 hours	Est 3 hours	Enjoying being involved in development work	Jan 2002
	7 hours	Est 1 hour	This will be my first experience of this conference	
Sept 2001	2 hours	1 hour	Worthwhile	Jan 2002
June 2001			Still not sure about some aspects of the guidelines	June 2002

Continuing Professional Development Plan/Record   (Draft Exemplar)

CPD Activity (Brief Description)	Planned CPD Activity Date(s) and Source					
	SDP	SD and R	Collective Time Activities	Devt. Day Prog	Other	
Child protection				12 Oct 2001		
Inclusive Education & Support for Learning				9 Nov 2001		
SDP Audit/self evaluation workshop	4 Mar 2002			4 Mar 2002		
Lead working group on Writing			Aug to Dec 2001			
Ian Smith/Teaching for Effective Learning (Twilight)		Jan 23 2002				
Presentation on Classroom Visits				4 Mar 2002		
NOF Training	Sept March 2002					
Preparation for SDandR/ SD andR discussion		June 2002				
Advisory Service course on mental maths	Sept 2001					
Interview skills workshop		Feb 2002				
Review of Assessment (Department meetings)			Sept/ May	May 2002		
New guidelines on environmental studies (Private reading)	Aug 2001					

Completion Date(s)	Time to Complete (Hours)		Comments/Evaluations	Date(s) of Review of CPD Plan/Record (SD and R Discussions)
	Within 35 hr week	Outwith 35 hr week		
12 Oct 2001	2 hours		Education Resources procedures worthwhile, reassuring	June 2002
9 Nov 2001	2 hours		Education Resources policy statement, challenging	June 2002
4 Mar 2002	3 hours		Good exercise, identified staff concerns	June 2002
Dec 2001	5 hours	5 hours	Enjoyed this group. Should ensure more consistent practice	June 2002
Jan 2002	5 hours		See evaluation sheet	June 2002
4 Mar 2002	1 hour		Better understanding of what classroom visiting is about	June 2002
May 2002	5 hours	20 hours	See Evaluation sheet	June 2002
June 2002	1 hour	2 hours	Good discussion	June 2002
Delayed Nov 2001				June 2002
Cancelled				
June 2002	5 hours	2 hours	Welcomed opportunity to share our concerns and practices	June 2002
June 2001		1 hour	Still not sure about some aspects of the guidelines	June 2002

References

Chapter 1

Adey, P., Hewitt, G., Hewitt, J., and Landau, N. (2004) *The Professional Development of Teachers: Theory and Practice* (London: Kluwer Academic Publishers).

Barber, M. (1996) *The Learning Game: Arguments for an Educational Revolution* (London: Victor Gollancz).

Bryce, T. G. K., and Humes, W. M. (eds.) (2003) *Scottish Education. Second Edition: Post-devolution* (Edinburgh: Edinburgh University Press).

Christie, D. (2003) 'Professional Studies in Initial Teacher Education' in Bryce and Humes (2003: p. 931–41).

DFES (2003) *Excellence and Enjoyment* (London: HMSO).

Fullan, M., and Hargreaves, A. (1993) *Teacher Development and Educational Change* (London: Routlege Falmer).

Fullan, M. (1995) 'The limits and potential of professional development', in T. R. Gusky and M. Huberman (1995) *Professional development in education: New Paradigms and Practices* (New York: Teachers' College Press).

Fullan, M. (2001) *Leading in a Culture of Change* (San Francisco, CA: Jossey Bass).

Hartley, D., and Roger, A. (eds.) (1990) *Curriculum and Assessment in Scotland: a Policy for the 90s* (Edinburgh: Scottish Academic Press).

Hoyle, E. (1974) 'Professionalism, professionality and control in teaching', in Houghton, V., McHugh, R. and Morgan, C. (eds.) *Management in Education* (London: Ward Lock).

Houghton, V., McHugh, R., and Morgan, C. (Eds.) *Management in Education* (London: Ward Lock).

Hustler, D., McNamara, O., Jarvis, J., Londra, M., Campbell, A., and Howson, J. (2003) *Teachers' Perspectives of Continuing Professional Development: DFES Research Brief no. 429* (London: DFES).

Kirk, G. (2003) 'Teacher Education Institutions', in Bryce and Humes (2003).

Lennon, F. (2003) 'Organisation and Management in the Secondary School Institutions', in Bryce and Humes (2003: p. 419–28).

McBer, H. (2001) 'Research into Teacher Effectiveness', in Banks and Mayes (2001: p. 193–209).

Menmure, J. (2003) 'SCOTCAT and SCQF Arrangements', in Bryce and Humes (2003: p. 974–81).

Munro, J. (2001) 'Learning more about learning improves teacher effectiveness', in Banks and Mayes (2001: p. 210–25).

Purdon, A. (2003) The Professional Development of Teachers in Bryce and Humes (2003: p. 942–51).

Sachs, J. (2003) *The Activist Teaching Profession* (Buckingham: Open University Press).

Scheerens, J., and Bosker, R. (1997) *The Foundation of Educational Effectiveness* (London: Pergamon).

Schon, D. (1987) *Educating the Reflective Practitioner* (San Francisco, CA: Jossey-Bass).

SED (Scottish Education Department) (1965) *Primary Education in Scotland* (*The Primary Memorandum*) (Edinburgh: HMSO).

SED (1977) *The Curriculum in the Third and Fourth Years of the Scottish Secondary School* (*The Munn Report*) (Edinburgh: HMSO).

SED (1977) *Assessment for All* (*The Dunning Report*) (Edinburgh: HMSO).

SEED (Scottish Executive Education Department) (2002) *Continuing Professional Development* (Edinburgh: HMSO).

SEED (2001) *A Teaching Profession for the 21st Century* (*The McCrone Report)* (Edinburgh: HMSO).

Stoll, L., and Fink, D. (1996) *Changing our Schools: Linking School Effectiveness and School Improvement* (Buckingham: Open University Press).

'What CPD did you do this year?', *Times Educational Supplement Scotland*, 21 May 2004.

Chapter 2

Dunning Report – see Chapter 1 references.

Harrison, M. M., and Marker, W. B. (1996) *Teaching the Teachers* (Edinburgh: John Donald Publishers).

Mortimer, G. (1996) 'Inservice and Special Needs', in Harrison and Marker (1996: p. 122–33).

McCrone Report – see Chapter 1 references.

Munn Report – *see* Chapter 1 references.

Munro, N., (2004) 'Effect and Efficiency beyond the finish line', *Times Educational Supplement Scotland*, 21 May 2004.

Primary memorandum – *see* Chapter 1 references.

Purdon, A. (2003) – *see* Chapter 1 references.

University of Strathclyde (2004) *Professional Development Unit: Catalogue of Providers* (Glasgow: University of Strathclyde).

Chapter 3

Bone, T. (1992) as quoted in Boyd (2004).

Boyd, B. (2004) 'Letting a Hundred Flowers Blossom', Ph.D. Thesis (University of Glasgow).

CCC (Consultative Council on the Curriculum) (1986) *Education 10–14 in Scotland* (Dundee: Consultative Council on the Curriculum).

Chirnside, A. (1992) as quoted in Boyd (2004).

Gow, L., and McPherson, A. F. (1980) *Tell Them from Me: Scottish School Leavers Write about School and Life Afterwards* (Aberdeen: Aberdeen University Press).

Humes, W. M. (1986) *The Leadership Class in Scottish Education* (Edinburgh: John Donald Publishers).

McPherson, A., and Raab, C. (1988) *Governing Education* (Edinburgh: Edinburgh University Press).

The Munn Report – *see* Chapter 1 references.

The Primary Memorandum – *see* Chapter 1 references.

SED (1963) *From School to Further Education* (*The Brunton Report*) (Edinburgh: HMSO).

SED (1977) *Truancy and Indiscipline in Schools in Scotland* (*The Pack Report*) (Edinburgh: HMSO)

Chapter 4

Department for Education and Science (1978) *Special Educational Needs: Report of the Committee of Enquiry into the Education of Handicapped Children and Young People* (*The Warnock Report*) (London: HMSO).

Farquharson, E. A. (1990) 'History, Culture and the Pedagogy of the Primary Memorandum', in *Scottish Educational Review* 22 (1) No. 1:36.

Fullan, M. G. (1992) *Successful School Improvement* (Buckingham: Open University Press).

Gatherer, W. (1989) *Curriculum Development in Scotland* (Professional Issues in Education) series (Edinburgh: Scottish Academic Press).

Hamill, P. and Boyd, B. (2000) *Striving for Inclusion; the Development of Integrated Support Systems for Young People with Social, Emotional and Behavioural Difficulties* (Glasgow: University of Strathclyde).

Hamill, P. and Boyd, B. (2001) *Inclusive Education: Taking the Initiative* (Glasgow: University of Strathclyde).

Hamill, P., Boyd, B., and Grieve, A. (2002) *Inclusion: principles into practice* (Glasgow: University of Strathclyde).

SED (1947) *Primary Education: A Report of the Advisory Council on Education in Scotland* (Edinburgh: HMSO).

SED (1981) *Learning and Teaching in Primary 4 and Primary 7* (Edinburgh: HMSO).

SED (1994) *Higher Skill – Opportunity for All* (Howie) (Edinburgh: HMSO).

Chapter 5

Boyd, B. and Lawson, J. (2004) 'Guidance Matters: a pupil perspective on guidance within a Scottish Council' *Improving Schools* volume 7 number 2.

Brown, S. (1989) 'How do teachers talk about and evaluate their own teaching?' *Spotlight 12* (Edinburgh: Scottish Council for Research in Education).

Christie, D. (2003) 'Competences, benchmarks and standards in teaching', in Bryce an Humes (2003).

Fullan, M. G. (1999) *Change Forces: the Sequel* (London: The Falmer Press).

Gow, L. and McPherson, A. (1980) *Tell Them from Me* (Aberdeen: Aberdeen Univeristy Press).

GTCS (General Teaching Council for Scotland) (2000) *Quality Assurance in Initial Teacher Education* (Edinburgh: HMSO).

GTCS (2003) *Achieving the Standard for Full Registration* (Edinburgh: HMSO).

Hamill, P. and Boyd, B. (2000) – *see* Chapter 4 references.

Hargreaves, A. and Hopkins, D. (1993) *The Empowered School* (London: Cassell).

Hartley, D. (1985) 'Bureaucracy and Professionalism: the new 'hidden curriculum' for teachers in Scotland', *Journal of Education for Teaching* 11/2: 107–19.

Kolb, D. A. (1976) *Learning Style Inventory: Technical Manual* (Englewood Cliffs, NJ: Prentice Hall).

MacBeath, J., Boyd, B., Rand, J., and Bell, S. (1986) *Schools Speak for Themselves* (Glasgow: Quality in Education Centre University of Strathclyde).

O'Brien, J., Murphy, D., and Draper, J. (2003) *School Leadership* (Policy and Practice in Education series) (Edinburgh: Dunedin Academic Press).

Rudduck, J., Chaplin, R., and Wallace, G. (eds.) (1996) *School Improvement: What Can Pupils Tell Us?* (London: David Fulton Publishers).

Schon, D. A. (1983) *The Reflective Practitioner* (New York: Basic Books).

SEED (2000) *Quality Assurance in Initial Teacher Education* (Edinburgh: HMSO).

SEED (2000) *Standard for Headship in Scotland* (Edinburgh: HMSO).

SEED (2002) *Standard for Chartered Teacher* (Edinburgh: HMSO).

Whitaker, P. (1993) *Managing Change in Schools* (Oxford: Oxford University Press).

Chapter 6

Blane, D. (2004) 'Keep learning and kepp up to date', *TESS* 12 Mar 2004.

Goodlad, J. I. (1990) *Education Renewal: Better Schools, Better Teachers* (San Francisco, CA: Jossey-Bass Publishers).

Hartley, D. (1985) – *see* Chapter 5 references.

Kirk, G., Beveridge, W., and Smith, I. (2003) *The Chartered Teacher* (Policy and Practice in Education series) (Edinburgh: Dunedin Academic Press).

The McCrone Report – *see* Chapter 1 references.

Munro, N. (2004) 'Effect and efficiency beyond the finish line', *TESS*, 21 May 2004.

NCITT (1979) *The Future of Inservice Training in Scotland* (The Green Report) (HMSO: Edinburgh).

SEED(1997) *A Framework for Leadership and Management Development in Scottish Schools* (Edinburgh: HMSO).

Sutherland, Sir Stewart (1997) 'Report 10 – Teacher Education and Training: A Study' (The Sutherland Report) in National Committee of Enquiry into Higher Education *Higher Education in the Learning Socity* Report of the National Committee (Norwich: HMSO).

Chapter 7

Adey, P. (2004) *The Professional Development of Teachers* (London: Kluer Academic Publishers).

Brown, S. (1989) – *see* Chapter 5 references.

Conlon, T. (2004) *A Failure of Delivery: The United Kingdom's New Opportunities Fund Programme of Teacher Training in Information and Technology*, Journal of In-Service Education Vol 30 No 1: pp. 115–139

Goodlad, J. I. (1990) *Education Renewal: Better Schools, Better Teachers* (San Francisco, CA: Jossey-Bass Publishers).

Fullan, M. G. (1992) *Successful School Improvement* (Buckingham: Open University Press).

Fullan, M. (2003) – *Change Forces with a Vengeance* (London: Routledge Falmer).

Hopkins, D and Lagerweij, N. (1996) 'The school improvement knowledge base', in Reynolds, D., Bollen, R., Creemers, B., Hopkins, D., Stoll, L., and Lagerweij, N. (eds.) (1996) *Making good schools* (New York: Teachers' College Press).

MacBeath *et al.* (1996) – *see* Chapter 5 references.

The McCrone Report – *see* Chapter 1 references.

Rosenholtz , S. (1989) *Teachers' Workplace: The Social Organisation of Schools* (New York: Longman).

Ruddock, J. *et al.* (1996) – *see* Chapter 5 references.

Rutter, M., Maugham, B., Mortimore, P. ,and Ouston, J. (1979) *Fifteen Thousand Hours* (London: Open Books).

Stallings, J. A. (1989) 'School achievement effects and staff development: what are some critical factors?', Paper presented at the Annual Meeting of the American Educational Research Association, San Francisco, CA, Mar 1989.

Chapter 8

Doyle, W. (1977) 'Paradigms for research on teacher effectiveness', in L. Shulman (ed.) *Review of Research in Education* (5: 163–98) (Washington: AERA).

Guskey, T. R. (2000) *Evaluating Professional Development: New Paradigms and Practices* (New York: Teachers' College Press).

Hall, J. and O'Conner, K. (1994) *How to set your own quality standards* (TES)

HMI (2000) *Educating the Whole Child* (HMSO: Edinburgh).

Ward, C., and Craigen, L. (1999) *Cooperative Learning: A Resoource Book* (Durham District School Board, Ontario).

Chapter 9

Bennet, N. (1976) *Teaching Styles and Pupil Progress* (London: Open Books).

Black, P., and Wiliam, D. (2000) *Inside the Black Box* (London: NFER-Nelson).

Caldwell, B. J., and Spinks, J. M. (1988) *The Self-Managing School* (Lewes: Falmer Press).

Clark, D. (1992) 'Search for a more effective future', in Gideonse, H. (ed.) (1992: 269–95) *Teacher Education Policy: Narrative Stories, and Cases* (Albany, NY: SUNY Press).

Coleman, J. S., Campbell, E. Q., Hobson, C. J. *et al.* (1966) *Equality of Educational Opportunity* (Washington DC: Office of Education).

Delamont, S. and Galton, M. (1986) *Inside the Secondary Classroom* (London: Routledge and Kegan Paul).

'Don't ask parents to do the impossible', *TESS* 17 Sept 2004.

Elmore, R. (2002) 'Hard questions about practice', *Educational Leadership* 59(8): 22–5.

Fullan, M. and Hargreaves, A. (1992) *What's worth fighting for in your school?* (New York NY: Teachers College Press).

Fullan, M. (2003) – *see* Chapter 7 references.

Goodlad, J. I. (1990) – *see* Chapter 7 references.

Hargreaves, A. and Fullan, M. (1992) *Understanding Teacher Development* (New York: Teachers College Press).

Hoban, G. (2002) *Teacher Learning for Educational Change* (Buckingham: Open University Press).

Howey, K. (1995) 'The United States: the context for restructuring and reconceptualision of teacher preparation', in Wideen, M. and Grimmett, P. (eds.) (1995: 19–33) *Changing Times in Teacher Education* (Washington DC: Falmer Press).

Jencks, C. *et al.* (1972) *Inequality: A Reassessment of the Effect of Family and Schooling in America* (New York, NY: Basic Books).

Lipman, M. (1991) *Thinking in Education* (Cambridge: Cambridge University Press).

MacBeath *et al.* – *see* Chapter 5 references.

The McCrone Report – *see* Chapter 1 references.

Reeves, J., Forde, C., O'Brien, J., Smith, P., and Tomlinson, H. (2002) *Performance Management in Education: Improving Practice* (London: Paul Chapman Publishing).

Reiman, A. J., and Thies-Sprinthall (1999) *Supervision and Mentoring for Teacher Development* (New York: Longman).

Rutter, M. *et al.* – *see* Chapter 7 references.

SEED (1997) *New Community Schools: a Prospectus* (Edinburgh: HMSO).

Stacey, R. (2001) *Complex Response Processes in Organisations* (London: Routlege).

Teachers for a New Era http://carnegie.org/sub/program/teachers_prospectus.html

Chapter 10

Boyd, B. and Bowes, K. (1996) *Breaking Down the Barriers: A Report on the Home School Employment Partnership* (Glasgow: University of Strathdyde).

Craft, A. (2000) *Continuing Professional Development* (London: Open University Press).

MacBeath *et al.* – *see* Chapter 5 rerferences.

Naisbit, J. and Aburdene, P. (1990) *Megatrends 2000: The next Ten Years – Major Changes in your Life and World* (London: Sedgwick and Jackson).

Nisbet, J. and Shucksmith, J. (1986) *Learning Strategies* (London: Routledge and Kegan Paul).

Rutter, M. *et al.* – *see* Chapter 7 rerferences.

Further Reading

Atkinson, T., and Claxton, G. (2000) 'Introduction', in T. Atkinson and G. Claxton (eds.) *The Intuitive Practitioner: On the value of not always knowing what one is doing* (Buckingham: Open University Press).

Banks, F., and Mayes, A.S . (2001) *Early Professional Development for Teachers* (London: David Fulton Publishers in association with Open University).

Chitty, C., and Simon, B. (eds.) (2001) *Promoting Comprehensive Education in the 21st Century* (Stoke on Trent: Trentham Books).

Gage, N. L. (1978) *The Scientific Basis of the Art of Teaching* (New York: Teachers' College Press).

McBer, H. cited in, The Open University (1992) 'Making Sense of Management', Unit 1 of E629 *Managing Educational Change* (Milton Keynes: The Open University).

Index